Essays by Drs. Morsi Saad El-Din, Gamal Mokhtar, Gawdat Gabra & Soad Maher

CAIRO
the Site & the History

الـقـاهـرة

CAIRO, The Site & The History
Published by
Stacey International
128 Kensington Church Street, London W8 4BH
Telex 298768 STACEY G

Consulting Editor : Dr Marsi Saad El-Din
Photography : Harri Peccinotti
Editor : Gregory Vitiello
Design : Derek Birdsall

This edition first published in the United Kingdom
by Stacey International, 1988
© Mobil Oil Egypt (S.A.E.)

British Library Cataloguing-in-Publication Data

Cairo : the site and the history
   1. Cairo (Egypt) – History
   1. Vitiello, Gregory
   962'.16   DT148

   ISBN 0-905743-55-5

Produced by Omnific Studios
Set in Van Dijck series 203
Printed by Balding + Mansell International Ltd, Great Britain

*Cover : Under the floodlights, and surrounded by darkness,
the Giza Sphinx and Pyramids are among history's most mysterious
and majestic sights.*

CONTENTS

PREFACE

Cairo, like any great city, is more than the sum of its parts. Over 5,000 years, many civilizations have asserted themselves; some have left mere traces in the sand, while others have left their indelible marks. It is these marks – these pyramids, obelisks, churches, mosques and palaces – that remind us of Cairo's past and that animate its present.

Fortunately, the past – of Cairo and of all of Egypt – is being restored to us through the herculean efforts of the Egyptian Government. We applaud the Government for all it is doing, and we urge the international community to support this effort since Egypt's heritage is a legacy to the world.

In the same spirit, through this book on Cairo, we celebrate the city's past. We also celebrate what Cairo has *become* – the complex living city of today.

It is a city we know and appreciate. Ever since Mobil came to Egypt 85 years ago, we have been based in Cairo. We have been involved in the nation's cultural life as sponsors of such projects as the Pegasus Prize for Egyptian Literature and *The Genius of Arab Civilization*. With this book on *Cairo, the Site and the History*, we are proud to continue our appreciation of this rich culture – and specifically the culture of Cairo.

We are especially fortunate in having assembled such a distinguished creative team: consulting editor Dr. Morsi Saad El-Din, art director Derek Birdsall, photographer Harri Peccinotti, and our outstanding group of authors – all Egyptians, and all leading scholars in their fields – Dr. Gamal Mokhtar, Dr. Gawdat Gabra and Dr. Soad Maher. I thank them all.

A special dedication must go to Mr. Oreste de Gaspari, former Chairman of Mobil Oil Egypt, who initiated this book.

Leslie B. Rogers III
Chairman
Mobil Oil Egypt (S.A.E.)

CONTENTS

PREFACE

Cairo, like any great city, is more than the sum of its parts. Over 5,000 years, many civilizations have asserted themselves; some have left mere traces in the sand, while others have left their indelible marks. It is these marks – these pyramids, obelisks, churches, mosques and palaces – that remind us of Cairo's past and that animate its present.

Fortunately, the past – of Cairo and of all of Egypt – is being restored to us through the herculean efforts of the Egyptian Government. We applaud the Government for all it is doing, and we urge the international community to support this effort since Egypt's heritage is a legacy to the world.

In the same spirit, through this book on Cairo, we celebrate the city's past. We also celebrate what Cairo has *become* – the complex living city of today.

It is a city we know and appreciate. Ever since Mobil came to Egypt 85 years ago, we have been based in Cairo. We have been involved in the nation's cultural life as sponsors of such projects as the Pegasus Prize for Egyptian Literature and *The Genius of Arab Civilization*. With this book on *Cairo, the Site and the History*, we are proud to continue our appreciation of this rich culture – and specifically the culture of Cairo.

We are especially fortunate in having assembled such a distinguished creative team: consulting editor Dr. Morsi Saad El-Din, art director Derek Birdsall, photographer Harri Peccinotti, and our outstanding group of authors – all Egyptians, and all leading scholars in their fields – Dr. Gamal Mokhtar, Dr. Gawdat Gabra and Dr. Soad Maher. I thank them all.

A special dedication must go to Mr. Oreste de Gaspari, former Chairman of Mobil Oil Egypt, who initiated this book.

Leslie B. Rogers III
Chairman
Mobil Oil Egypt (S.A.E.)

FOREWORD

Nothing gives me more pleasure than to see a new book published about Cairo. This is not merely because I happen to be the Governor of Egypt's capital, but because in Cairo I can perceive the whole of Egypt, its people, its history and its culture.

Despite overpopulation and the common problems from which all great cities suffer, Cairo has its unique charm.

In this glorious city, I always smell the fragrance of the past and witness the greatness of our ancestors.

In fact, one of my main preoccupations is the restoration of Cairo's heritage. This is no easy job since most of the monuments are in residential areas, while the monuments of the pharaohs and their relics are in the desert where the sand acts as a good preserver.

When the Egyptian Ministry of Culture decided in 1969 to celebrate the millenary of Cairo, two points of view emerged. One declared that Cairo the site was over 6,000 years old, as capital of Egypt; that site of course covered Memphis, Fustat, Al-Askar, Al-Qatai, and finally Cairo. The other point of view, meanwhile, wanted to concentrate on the period in which the capital bore the name of Cairo, and which exceeds 1,000 years.

I am glad to see that this book supports the first point of view, since to me, Cairo is a conglomeration of all previous capitals, and its character and culture are the sum total of all its successive civilizations: Pharaonic, Greek, Roman, Coptic and Islamic.

What gives Cairo its prestige is the position it occupies as the gateway between two continents and two seas. This position, coupled with the continuity of its history, has permitted Cairo to be one of the world's greatest and most ancient capitals.

In supporting this book, Mobil Oil Egypt has made an important contribution to our city and our culture, which we should appreciate.

Yousef Sabri Abou Taleb, Governor of Cairo

INTRODUCTION *Dr. Morsi Saad El-Din*

Some may think that it is presumptuous to produce a new book about Cairo. Dozens of books have been already written and published about this great capital of Egypt. When the Egyptian Ministry of Culture celebrated the millennium of Cairo in 1969, savants, historians and men of letters came from all over the world to pay homage to this great city, the mother of the world, as it is called.

Looking through the list of specialists who submitted papers, one cannot but feel a sense of pride, as an Egyptian, to see these great men from Britain, France, Italy, East and West Germany, Hungary, the United States and the Soviet Union contributing their share of knowledge about our capital.

True, many books have been written about Cairo, dealing with different aspects of her life, like Stanley Lane-Poole's famous book *Cairo − Sketches of its History, Monuments and Social Life*, or Desmond Stewart's popular book *Cairo . . . Mother of the World*, to mention a few.

However, this book is different in two ways: It is written not by one writer but by a group of writers, all specialists and each of them dealing with his or her specific field. Second, all the contributors are Egyptians who, some may say, may be prejudiced in favor of their own capital. It is true that there is no such thing as objective writing when it comes to one's own country. But, being the specialists they are, our contributors have managed to doff their cloaks of subjectivity. Examples of this can be found in their descriptions and at times criticisms of some pharaohs, kings, sultans and princes who ruled Egypt.

What is also new in this book is the way the emergence of Cairo has been traced from its prehistoric times, and the reader will get to know the geography and physical formation of the city, the role of the desert and the Valley of the Nile in shaping her features, as well as the character of her people. He will also be able to follow the development of Cairo's topography, its geological history − in short, all that nature has endowed the city with, and deprived her of.

Cairo is the throbbing heart of Egypt. No wonder Egyptians always refer to it as *Masr* (Egypt) rather than *Al-Kahira*, which is "Cairo" in Arabic. The use of the word *Masr* clearly reflects the central role of Cairo in the very history of the country.

Going through the book, the reader will no doubt grasp a very significant characteristic of Cairo, the continuity of her history and development. This strongly linked chain of events and occurrences has helped to form the character of the city.

Cairo has always been like a melting pot where all ages, all dynasties, all invaders mixed together and produced something that is uniquely Cairo. Different travelers to Egypt have been struck by the way the different arts − Pharaonic, Greek, Roman, Coptic, Byzantine and Islamic − have been interwoven to produce a unity in all artistic manifestations. Mosques reveal Byzantine and Coptic influences, while churches abound with Arab and Islamic motifs. Above all, we find the influence of Pharaonic Egypt acting as a catalyst that helps to produce the right substance in the melting pot of Cairo.

The title of the book *Cairo, the Site and the History* has not been chosen at random. Although we refer to our city as Cairo, which only recently celebrated its 1,000th year of existence, what we actually mean is the site where Cairo was and still is. When the pharaohs chose it as their capital, it was not Cairo but Memphis. When the Arabs came into Egypt and looked for a capital, it was approximately the same site as Memphis. They called it *Al-Fustat*, meaning tent, and used it as barracks for their troops.

So did Salah el-Din and all the other kings and sultans who followed him. Cairo was kept as the capital, the center of political, social and cultural activities, but each king or sultan had something to add to it, especially in the way of art and architecture. Each dynasty left its indelible mark on Cairo, not only architecturally but also politically and religiously. Each king, sultan or emir had his idiosyncrasies that were reflected in his contributions. A sultan who was fond of flowers gave his orders to cultivate parks and gardens. An emir who was treated in a *Bamaristan* (a hospital) in Damascus had similar institutions built upon his return to Cairo.

But all of them had one thing in common: they built mosques with schools attached, and sometimes medical clinics. The central task of the schools, apart from teaching the Quran and Arabic, was to perpetuate the religious tenets of their respective sects. Schools during the Fatimids taught Shia principles while the Ayyubids spread through the school principles of the four Sunni *imams*.

In essence, there has never been one Cairo, but many, each with her own physical features and characteristics. These different Cairos can still be seen in our modern city. Shia mosques like Al-Hussein and Sayyeda Zeinab can be seen side by side with mosques built by Sunni dynasties. Yet all are houses of God and of worship, and it is a common sight to see Shia tourists from other Arab countries visiting these mosques.

Most cities have their lore, a mixture of fact and fiction. Of this, Cairo has an abundance. One of the legends about Cairo, as told by a number of Islamic specialists, relates to the choice of the site by Gawhar Al-Sikelli. It is said that Gawhar summoned the astrologers and told them to choose a propitious moment for the foundation of the city, so that the Fatimid dynasty would never be dispossessed. All along the lines of trenches dug to receive the foundations of the walls were fixed posts, connected by cords, on which bells were hung. At the most propitious moment, the astrologers would send a signal down the line, and the bells would ring. The astrologers told the workmen to stand by, ready to throw into the trenches stones and mortar that had been placed within their reach; but before the right moment arrived, a crow alighted on the cord, the bells tinkled, and the workmen, thinking that astrologers had given the signal, set to work. At this moment, the planet Mars was in the ascendant. This planet was for the Arabs *Qaher el-Fala* (the conqueror of the galaxy) and they considered this an evil omen.

While most people who wrote about Cairo never doubted the authenticity of this legend, K.A.Creswell tends to disbelieve it since the same story originated years before, almost word for word, concerning Alexander's building of Alexandria.

There were many descriptions of life in Cairo during the different phases of its development and under the many rulers who sat on the throne of Egypt. But in spite of this, Cairo remained the same. Though there were additions and extensions, new buildings and gardens, as Lane-Poole puts it:

". . . Cairo is still to a great degree the city of the Arabian nights. We can still shut our eyes to the hotels and restaurants, the dusty grass pots and the villas of the European quarter and turn away to wonder at the labyrinth of narrow lanes which intersect the old part of the city, just as they did in the days of the Mameluke sultans."

The time of the Mamelukes is supposed to have been a time of luxury, extravagance and festivals. They are believed to have made the best of their festivals. They even allowed their servants to go out and amuse themselves in the gaiety of the illuminated streets.

"Hung with silk and satin, and filled with dancers, jugglers, and revellers, fantastic figures, the oriental punch, and the Chinese shadows."

This sounds like a description of carnivals as we know them in modern times. It is also known that during the rule of the Mameluke Sultan Beybars, a concert was held every night in the Citadel. There, a torch was gently moved to and fro to keep the

time. Lane-Poole believes that Mameluke Cairo was the setting of the Arabian Nights. "Whatever the origin and scene of the stories, the manners and customs are drawn from the society of Cairo in the days of the Mamelukes," Lane-Poole writes.

The Mameluke period saw the emergence of the first and only queen to rule an Islamic land. After the death of her husband, Sultan Saleh Ayoub, in the middle of his war with the Crusaders, Shagaret El-Dor (tree of pearls) assumed power. She kept the death of her husband secret until the Egyptian armies were able to rout the French and take their king prisoner. Her reign did not last long: Her female slaves beat her to death with bath clogs.

Another legend concerns Mohammad Ali's massacre of the Mamelukes. He invited them to dinner at the Citadel, and while they were enjoying a meal and entertainment, Mohammad Ali ordered them to be killed. The story has it that one of the Mamelukes managed to escape the massacre and vault on his horse over the walls of the Citadel. Dragomen used to show tourists the imprints of the hooves. But it has been proven that this is more fiction than fact. It is believed that the Mameluke who survived distrusted Mohammad Ali's invitation and never went to the Citadel at all. Yet the story is still told and still believed.

Among the many legends associated with Memphis is that of Queen Nitocris of the 6th dynasty, who was buried in the Pyramid of Menkara. According to legend, she was beautiful, with rosy cheeks, slender body and delicate feet. The story is told that when Queen Nitocris was relaxing at the side of her emerald pool, a bird of prey swooped down and snatched one of her golden sandals. When the bird realized that it wasn't food, it dropped the sandal into the garden of Rhadopis. The prince fell in love with the owner of the sandal and asked his men to find her. As in the story of Cinderella, they went from house to house trying to fit the sandal to a human foot, until finally they found Nitocris. Even today, popular fancy imagines a beautiful woman who haunts the Pyramid of Menkara and lures bewildered travelers to their doom.

Another legend is associated with Matarya, a suburb near Heliopolis, known as the city of the sun. Heliopolis had the most ancient university, the forerunner of European schools. According to Lane-Poole: "Here in all probability, Moses was instructed by the priests of Ra in all the wisdom of Egyptians. Here, too, Herodotus cross-questioned the same priesthood with varying success. Here Plato came to study and Euduxus the

Mathematician to learn astronomy, and here Strabo was shown the houses where famous Greeks had lived."

Of this seat of learning and focus of religion nothing remains but an obelisk. Beside the obelisk is an ancient sycamore, riven with age and hacked with numberless names beneath which, tradition has it, the Holy Family rested in their flight into Egypt, and which is now known as The Virgin Tree. Nearby is a spring of fresh water, which it is said became sweet because the child Jesus was bathed there. From the spots where the drops fell from His swaddling clothes, after they too had been washed in this sacred spring, sprang up balsam trees, which it was believed, flourished nowhere else.

There is no evidence for those fancies. But as Lane-Poole puts it: "The tradition is no more than a legend, yet there is no place in Egypt to which the visit of the Holy Family would be more fit, than to the almost deserted seat of learning."

القَـاهِـرَة

Lawrence Durrell, the author of the *Alexandria Quartet*, often wrote about what he called the genius of the place, or the spirit of the place. What he meant was that the place is the main manipulator of character, and that the geographical features of a country reflect on its people.

Before dealing with the geography of Cairo, we should know something about the geography of Egypt, and its regional personality. This personality is not the work of geography alone, but of history as well as geology, archaeology and even anthropology.

Egypt is often called the land of paradoxes, the land of anomalies. It is at the same time a river land and a desert land. It is an example of a perfect river environment, or to be more specific, a flood environment. The river constitutes Egypt's very life; without it, there would be no Egypt. Herodotus said that Egypt was the token of the Nile. Indeed, Egypt *is* the Nile.

Egypt is a hydrological society, and it has one of the most complicated networks of irrigation canals. But it is also the largest desert country in the world. It is a land of agriculture, but no plants. It has no natural flora, no grass, no savanna, no forests. Its topography is a mixture of the natural and the artificial.

Egypt is a central country. It lies almost exactly in the center of the world. It is the only country where the Red Sea and

the Mediterranean meet, where the River Nile meets the Mediterranean. It is in two continents, Africa and Asia, and is the gateway to the Far East. It is an example of the reaction between the site and the situation. The site is the environment with all its perspective, while the situation is geographical. The size of Egypt's site is not always in ratio with its situation, lying, as it were, at the hub of the world.

The Valley is another feature of Egypt. Looking down from an airplane, one would see a green strip on both sides of the river, then abruptly the green ends and the spatial expanse of desert takes over. Life is concentrated in this green strip, and this led to the creation of political unity, to the centralization of power that gave Cairo, the capital, a concentration of power and to the establishment of the first bureaucracy in the world.

At first, the desert led to the isolation of Egypt, but it was also a defensive belt that allowed the country to live, during the first centuries, in a state of independence. This allowed Egypt to develop its civilization unhampered by outside invasion. Egypt's situation made it a meeting place of east and west, north and south, and one of the first countries to develop trade. The first empire in the world was formed in Egypt, but it was a peaceful, not an aggressive empire. It is often said that the River Nile made Egypt a land power, while its extended shores made it a sea power.

Egypt is part of what geographers call the Arab-Nubian mass, and as such, part of the great Sahara Shield or the African Shield. Egypt was formed gradually and continually as a result of a chain of long and complicated eras of sea flooding the land from the north, then receding again. This process continued over many centuries. The resulting deposits formed the land of Egypt.

But the Nile has always played an important role in the formation of the country. Geographic and geological maps show that the Nile does not run in the middle of the desert, but veers to the east. It is often said that had the Nile run more to the west the course of history would have changed.

The Nile in its long and difficult course from its source to its mouth covers varied geological areas. It is a typical example of what is termed differential erosion with a succession of ridges and valleys. Egypt's limestone soil was able to resist the erosion of the river. We have an example in the Muqattam hills, which have survived this erosion. Basalt is also a feature of Egypt's land and it is found in the mountainous woods east of Cairo.

There have been many theories about the formation of the

Nile, and questions have always been asked about the time and the nature of its emergence. A geologist named Blankenhorn claimed that a large river originating in ancient times used to flow into the sea. Over the ages that river eventually dried up. At the same time, the sea inundated the land and formed the present course of the river. He called it the Libyan Nile and regarded it as the grandfather of the present river.

A theory put forward by a geologist named Cailliand was that a dried-up course of a river west of the Nile – often referred to as "a river without water" – in the Western Desert was the origin of the Nile and it ran parallel to the present course.

If Egypt is the meeting place of east and west, north and south, Cairo is the meeting place of the Nile Valley and the Delta, the thin strip of green and the fan-shaped fertile land. Cairo can be regarded as the waist of the Valley, a hydrological knot where the Nile begins to branch out into two arms embracing the Delta between them.

To the east of Cairo we can see the Muqattam heights with their broken line of beige and khaki, their weather-beaten, eroded cliffs that once overlooked the Mediterranean before the Delta had begun to form. They are 550 feet above the Nile. This is the protective shield of Cairo. Desmond Stewart compares the Delta to an open hand, and where Cairo stands is the pulse, the wrist. Whoever controls this pulse can control both the Valley and the Delta.

But the Nile was not the only route. To the northwest of Cairo, around the Muqattam hills, one can see a broad waterless valley, Wadi Tumilat, which leads to the Isthmus of Suez. This was supposed to be the route taken by caravans and it linked Europe with the Red Sea across Egypt.

The Western Hills, the Libyan plateau, are the start of the Sahara.

Desmond Stewart compares the strategic position of Cairo to that of Troy. Cairo dominates the Nile, which is a waterway easy to navigate. With the development of Cairo, standing at the top of the Delta, its needs expanded and its central position was exploited further. Waterways were dug, making it possible to ship goods from the Nile to the Red Sea.

If we follow the development of Egypt's capitals from Pharaonic times, we can clearly see the importance of Cairo as a site.

Egyptian capitals began with Memphis, after the unification of the country by Menes. Right from the start, the builders of Memphis showed strategic sense. They built the city on the West Bank of the Nile. At that time, the Delta started to fan out a short distance north of where Memphis now is.

The city was then called Mit Rahira. After moving to Abydos (*Al Araba*), it returned to Memphis with the 3rd dynasty, where it continued as capital until the 8th dynasty when it moved to Aknasiu, then to Thebes where it lasted for 800 years.

The capital of Egypt continued to move, to Alexandria where it lasted for 1,000 years, and when the Arabs entered Egypt, Cairo became their capital, but under different names. This means that the first Egyptian capital was established in the Cairo area, and came full circle, ending there. The full life of Memphis/Cairo as a capital is over 2,500 years, of Alexandria, 1,000, and of Thebes 800. During Pharaonic times, the capital changed often, which means that the Pharaonic times were experimental. By the time the Arabs came, the importance of Cairo's site was well established, and its strategic value was recognized.

The movement of the seat of government from Alexandria, a coastal city, to an inland city like Cairo can be regarded as a manifestation of nationalism. The neck of the Delta, whether known as Memphis, Heliopolis, Fustat, Qatai or Cairo, was the natural site for a capital. As one writer puts it: "It was as if the site was chosen by the Gods." The site was like a magnet drawing to it all rulers. This also emphasizes the strong geographical centralization that would facilitate the administration of the whole country.

Cairo is an ancient, deeply rooted and noble city. It has a unique landscape, lying between two hanging curves of ancient history: the Pharaonic to the west and the Islamic to the east. In the Pyramids plateau at Giza, we find the remains of Pharaonic times, while at the Muqattam hills and at their feet we find Islamic Cairo, which still lives today. The city stretches in the lower part between the two curves, a point where the greater part of the history of Egypt is concentrated.

From the morphological point of view, Egypt is what geographers call "amphitheatral." It is, in fact, the last basin of the east and Upper Egypt, open from the north, to connect with the Delta gushing into it. In this sense it is similar to the morphology of the eastern part of Upper Egypt, as far as the elevation of the contours to the east are concerned. The area was always subjected to torrents from the desert and in many ways Cairo is a miniature of the whole valley.

Greater Cairo today is fan-shaped, narrow in the south, with

THE PHARAONIC ERA
Dr. Gamal Mokhtar

Cairo is the political, economic, administrative and cultural capital of Egypt, the largest city in Africa, the gateway to the Middle East, the heart of the Arab world, the entrance to, and at the same time the mouth of, the Nile – the world's most famous river . . . the city marked by the Giza Pyramids and guarded by the Great Sphinx. Yet until 40 years ago, it was scarcely visited by people for its glorious past and its fabulous treasures. But since World War II, the city has overflowed with visitors from every part of the world, and they have returned to their homes inspired beyond words.

Cairo, in addition to its 600 or more Islamic monuments, is flanked by two mother cities with their own ancient and glorious past: Memphis in the south and Heliopolis in the north. Memphis was founded by Menes, the first pharaoh of Egypt, and after becoming the capital, it continued for tens of centuries to be the center of administration and power. Heliopolis, on the other hand, gained its importance much earlier, in the predynastic period and then became the center of Egyptian culture, faith and inspiration for not less than 3,000 years.

Cairo itself includes thousands of Pharaonic monuments, brought from archaeological sites all over Egypt to be exhibited in the Cairo Museum, one of the most celebrated in the world. In the center of the city, in Ramses Square, stands a magnificent colossus of Ramses II, which was transferred from Memphis to be an ambassador representing the old capital in the modern one. Two fine obelisks, originally erected in the temple of Ramses II at Tanis in the Nile Delta, were restored and brought to Cairo, to be resurrected there. Moreover, the major historical sites of the Giza and Saqqara necropolises are within the limits of Greater Cairo or Metropolitan Cairo.

Ancient Egyptian monuments were nearly forgotten and completely neglected after the spread of Christianity and the entry of Islam into Egypt. But suddenly Ancient Egypt was resurrected, much interest began to arise, and a new branch of study called Egyptology was established. This study followed the appearance of the landmark publication *Description de l'Égypte* written by the French savants who had accompanied Bonaparte's military expedition to Egypt, and by the deciphering of hieroglyphics by Jean Francois Champollion at the beginning of the 19th century.

The Ancient Egyptian treasures were then collected and stored for the first time in a small building in Azbakiah garden in Cairo, and were subsequently transferred to the Citadel of Cairo. However, the entire collection was given to Austria by Abbas Pasha I, the ruler of Egypt when the Austrian Archduke Maximilian visited Egypt in 1855.

Three years later, after the French archaeologist Auguste Mariette was appointed general director of the Egyptian Department of Antiquities, he eventually succeeded in inducing the Egyptian authorities to construct a real museum to exhibit the Pharaonic artifacts. The dream was realized, first in 1863 in a museum in the suburb of Boulak, and then when the whole treasure was moved to Ismail Pasha Palace at Giza in 1890.

After some of Boulak's museum treasures had been shown in Paris in 1867, the Empress Eugénie, the wife of Napoleon III, sought them as a present from Khedive Ismail Pasha, the ruler of Egypt and a friend of the French royal family. But Mariette courageously and firmly refused her demand. It is therefore fitting that the garden of the Cairo Museum includes an elegant bronze statue of Mariette resting on his marble tomb, and bearing an inscription written in French citing "L'Égypte Reconnaissant."

The present neoclassical Cairo Museum, designed by the French architect Marcel Dourgnon, was inaugurated in 1902. It is located at the northern end of Tahrir (Liberation) Square in the heart of the main touristic area.

The Cairo Museum exhibits the world's largest collection of Pharaonic treasures, covering all of Ancient Egyptian history from prehistoric times until the Ptolemaic period. Although it is widely criticized as an overcrowded, inefficient museum, I believe that it succeeds in pointing out the richness of Ancient Egyptian civilization. At the same time, it reflects the peculiar mentality of the Ancient Egyptians, who left to us such crowded temples and tombs. In any case, current renovation and development work, including the addition of a new annex, will make for more suitable displays.

Among the masterpieces belonging to the Archaic Period and Old Kingdom are these artifacts from the Greater Cairo area:
King Zoser Statue, of painted limestone, found at Saqqara (3rd dynasty);
Seated statue of Khefren (Khafre), of diorite, found at Giza (4th dynasty);
Three triads of Mycerinus (Menkaure), of schist, found at Giza (4th dynasty);

Below: The desert at Dahshour, south of Saqqara, with Sneferu's pyramids in the background. Right: A fertile stretch of the Nile Valley at the edge of the desert and its enduring landmark, the Step Pyramid of Zoser at Saqqara.

its handle there and the wide parts of the fan to the north. This is the general shape of the fertile land of Egypt as well as of its capital.

From a purely geometrical point of view, Cairo is the center of gravity, the seat of government and administration. Cairo's position may not be at the exact middle between Upper and Lower Egypt as far as distance is concerned. But from the point of view of life, it is.

Egypt's population profile is like a pyramid whose top is the Cairo area. If we draw a circle with a radius of 75 kilometers with Cairo in its center, it will have one quarter of Egypt's population living in only one eighth of its size. This means that the human center of gravity is in Cairo.

Its population is a mix of people from all parts of Egypt, presenting a real and comprehensive sample of the population. It is estimated that one-third of Cairo's present population is from other governorates. This move toward urbanization, at one time a blessing, has now become a curse, creating for the Egyptian capital problems that are almost insurmountable.

With a flood environment and a hydrological society, centralization is essential. It is related to the functioning of the government. Irrigation means organization, which, in turn, led to political unity and was instrumental in teaching the people the fundamentals of civilization. It also created officialdom and central bureaucracy, which have become the stamp of Egyptian civilization. Bureaucracy is as old as Egyptian history. It began with the Pyramids, and the murals in the monuments show clearly the importance and esteem given to high officials and scribes. It played a serious role in Egypt and was, at that time, an organizing force. It was a blessing, and Egypt owed its prosperity to its bureaucracy. Without it, canals could not have been dug, and dams could not have been built.

Cairo was also the center of culture, the giver of life. It is often said that the whole of Egypt, indeed of the Arab world, dances to the tunes that are played in Cairo. Cairo is the very heart of Egypt, politically, economically and socially. This is why the fall of Cairo at the hands of invaders meant the fall of Egypt. This is why invaders always headed for Cairo. It is sometimes said that because of its situation, its size and its political importance, Cairo is the capital of the world.

The reader will notice that this book stops after Mohammad Ali, the founder of modern Egypt and consequently the founder of modern Cairo. Yet although he was a great innovator, Cairo still kept its original character and political traditions. The seat of government was still the Citadel where Mohammad Ali lived and carried out the affairs of state.

With the advent of Ismail the process of modernization became a process of Europeanization. He always declared that he wanted Egypt to be part of Europe, and he embarked on a process of construction unknown before: new palaces, boulevards, parks, and of course, the Opera House. But the country had to pay dearly for this, as a result of the loans Ismail obtained from European countries. One of his innovations was to move the seat of Government from the Citadel to Abdin palace.

We stopped with Mohammad Ali, but Cairo has been changing since then. With every positive new development have come new problems. In fact, Cairo's problems have drawn the attention of UNESCO and other organizations. Recently, a seminar pondered "The Expanding Metropolis: Coping with the Urban Growth of Cairo."

Dozens of Cairo lovers and experts attended the seminar and delivered a multitude of papers dealing with the complex issues facing Cairo. But, as I said, there are many faces of Cairo; indeed, many Cairos. Ours is different from theirs.

Seated scribe, of painted limestone, found at Saqqara (5th dynasty);

Standing statue of Ka-Aper (known as the statue of Sheikh el Balad), from sycamore wood, found at Saqqara (5th dynasty);

Niche of Dwarf Seneb and his family, of painted limestone, found at Giza (5th dynasty);

Two statues of Re Nefer, of painted limestone, found at Saqqara (5th dynasty).

The museum also contains some famous collections from the same period, such as the collection of Hemaka, an important official who lived in the time of King Den of the 1st dynasty, and whose tomb was discovered in Saqqara between the years 1931 and 1936. A splendid collection belonging to Queen Hetep Heres, the mother of King Cheops, was found in 1925 by chance in a well beside the pyramid of her son.

The Cairo Museum houses many masterpieces belonging to the Middle and New Kingdoms.

Among the wonderful collections from the Middle Kingdom is the jewelry of the royal princesses of the 12th dynasty, which was found at Dahshur and El Lisht. There are unique scenes, models of quotidian life, mostly made of wood; and also models of Egyptian and Nubian soldiers from the tomb of Mesehti at Asyuit (11th dynasty). Also included are maids bearing offerings, weavers' workshops, cattle-counting, fishermen at work, a carpentry shop and other expressions of everyday life more than 4,000 years ago.

The New Kingdom treasures exhibited in the Cairo Museum are the most fascinating and celebrated, especially those of King Tutankhamon, which were discovered in 1922 in his tomb in the Valley of the Kings in Western Thebes. It contains about 3,000 pieces – of which only 1,700 are exhibited, including such masterpieces as the golden coffin, the golden mask, the throne, his unique beds, chairs, boxes, statues and statuettes, jewels, chariots, canopies, alabaster vases and models.

القَاهِرَة

Until recently, Cairo – unlike many other big cities such as Rome, Paris, London, New York and Istanbul – had neither an obelisk nor any Pharaonic monument adorning its parks or squares. In 1958, however, the Egyptian Government decided to bring an obelisk to Cairo to be erected there. Since the archaeological site of Tanis (now called San El Hagar, in the northeast Delta) has more than 20 broken obelisks among the ruins of the Ramses II temple, the parts of one of those obelisks were collected, restored, reassembled and transferred to Cairo. This obelisk now stands on a modern pedestal in a small garden on Zamalek Island, on the western bank of the River Nile, facing central Cairo, and surrounded by some monuments that were brought from Tanis. The Zamalek obelisk, which dates back to 3,300 years ago, is nicely inscribed with hieroglyphics praising King Ramses II. Although it is more than 40 feet high, it looks rather short because of its proximity to a high minaret and to the Cairo Tower.

In 1984, the Egyptian Antiquities Department brought another obelisk from Tanis to the capital, to be re-erected on an artificial pedestal in the wide square facing Cairo International Airport – thus welcoming visitors and bidding farewell to those departing from Egypt. After it was reassembled, the obelisk proved to be well preserved. It is nearly 54 feet high and weighs about 120 tons. Each side of its pyramidion has a scene showing the king kneeling in front of a divinity; below the scene is a column of hieroglyphic inscriptions with one of the titles and names of Ramses II and words about his strength and his victories. The Egyptian Antiquities Department capped the obelisk with an artificial gilded brass pyramidion, imitating the Ancient Egyptian tradition of covering the top of the obelisk with a pyramidion of gold or electrum to reflect the light of the sun.

Assembled in the Museum or on public display, these artifacts offer a mere glimpse of the civilizations that once thrived in this area. Through our readings, and by visiting the sites themselves, we can learn more, not only of what these civilizations built but often of how they lived.

القَاهِرَة

The capital of the 13th nome (province) of lower Egypt was an ancient city named Iwn (the tower), called by the Greeks Heliopolis (the city of the sun) and mentioned biblically as "ON." It stood on a slightly raised ground to the east of the apex of Cairo. The only visible remnants are the standing obelisk of Senusert I (12th dynasty) and a few tombs hidden beneath a modern suburb of Cairo called Ein Shams, and a neighboring village named Kom El-Hisn. There must have been a spring of

Left: The standing obelisk of Senusert I from the 12th dynasty marks the site of ancient Heliopolis at Ein Shams, a modern suburb of Cairo.

Below: One of the few remnants of Memphis' greatness, this alabaster sphinx from the 18th or 19th dynasty was excavated in 1912 by the British archaeologist Flinders Petrie.

fresh water in the center of the city known as Ein Shams (the spring of the sun). The sun was believed in Pharaonic Egypt to bathe himself there everyday, morning and night.

Heliopolis played a great role in the social and intellectual life of Ancient Egypt. It also represents the most remote and glorious spiritual center in the history of mankind. Its traditions were mentioned in the Pyramid Texts, the most ancient religious texts of Ancient Egypt.

The sun was worshipped there under different names. One of them was Atum (the creator), who was the original god. He was later absorbed by Re, the Sun God of excellence. Re proclaimed for himself other aspects of the sun, such as Kheper (the god of creation) and Re Hor-m-Akhty (the god of the horizon), and he amalgamated the most important gods, Amon Khnum and Sobek, with himself. Akhenaton's heresy and philosophy were derived from the Heliopolitan doctrines.

Heliopolis Ennead, the first of the doctrines, encompassed the nine universal deities headed by Re, the sole creator. Among his offshoots were two couples: Geb (the earth) and Nut (the sky), and Shu (the atmosphere) and Tefnut (the moisture). Geb and Nut gave birth to Osiris, who married his sister Isis and was appointed as the first king of the fertile land (Egypt), and Seth, who married his sister Nephthys and became the king of the deserts surrounding Egypt.

Originally, the Egyptians – like most of the people of antiquity – used a lunar calendar. Some Egyptologists believe that the priests of Heliopolis perfected a solar calendar that was also connected with the Nile and the agricultural stages. Other scholars attribute the development of that calendar to the famous architect and astronomer Imhotep of the 3rd dynasty. According to that calendar, the year contained 365 days divided into 12 months, each 30 days long, plus five additional days at the end of the year. The months, in turn, were divided into three periods. The year had three seasons, each of which was four months long. The first season was called Akhet (inundation), which begins with the arrival of the flood water. The second season was called Perret (the going out of the water), equivalent to our winter. The third season was called Shmsu, during which the harvest began.

Later, the 12 months were given names, which are still kept in what we call "the Coptic Calendar," and is used by the farmers for agricultural purposes. This calendar, with some alterations by Julius Caesar, is the origin of the current Gregorian calendar.

The priests of Heliopolis were highly respected, and they were frequently visited by cultured Greeks searching for more knowledge, wisdom and science. Even Solon, the famous Greek lawmaker, and Pythagoras, the great scientist, probably stayed in Heliopolis sometime around the 6th century B.C. The priests had worshipped the Sun God since very ancient times, when the city already had its privilege and spiritual importance. The temples of the Sun God, who was worshipped under several names, were very influential in ideological, religious and even political affairs. The obelisks were first placed in sun temples of Heliopolis and were strongly linked to the sun cult.

Although the Heliopolis obelisk goes back to the Middle Kingdom, it is considered the oldest surviving one in the world. It is one of the pair of obelisks that stood in front of the Temple of the Sun God in Heliopolis. Its mate, which was reported on by Arab writers in the 12th and 13th centuries, has completely disappeared.

The surviving one is about 67 feet in height and 121 tons in weight. A single red granite block, it was brought from the quarries of Aswan. Each of its four sides has a column of inscription including the titles and names of the king, and some laudatory sentences. Much patience, genius and faith must have gone into its creation.

Two obelisks erected by Thutmoses III (18th dynasty) were removed from their original site and transferred during the Roman period to Alexandria, where they stayed until they left Egypt in modern times. One of them, now known as Cleopatra's Needle, was given to England and re-erected in London on the bank of the River Thames, while the other one stands beside the Metropolitan Museum in New York City's Central Park.

And so the Heliopolis obelisk is the only landmark of that important and influential ancient city, which at one time had many standing obelisks. But many were destroyed, others were taken abroad, and some may still be buried under the modern buildings that cover the entire area of ancient Heliopolis.

القَهـِـرة

In the Paleolithic period, stone-age men inhabited the site of what is now Cairo. We have found a great number of flint implements, particularly from the Atarian culture of the late Paleolithic, mainly in the Abassia desert and the Gebel El-Asfar (yellow mountain) on the outskirts of Cairo.

The only predynastic settlements in the area were found on the eastern bank of the Nile facing Memphis. These settlements, dating to the era between 3700 and 3100 B.C., are El-Omari near Helwan, and Maadi, located eight miles northwest of it.

Memphis, one of the oldest capitals in the world and the first capital of United Egypt, lay about 15 miles to the south of Giza and covered an enormous expanse, which is now limited to the area around a modern village called Mit Rahina.

Its original name in the time of Menes was *Inb hd*, which means The White Wall. Several centuries later, it became known as *Mn Nefer* – after the name of the Pyramid of Pepi I, the second pharaoh of the 6th dynasty – which is the origin of the Greek name Memphis and the Arabic name *Menf*. Its location, between Lower and Upper Egypt and near the branching of the Nile, made it ideal for establishing a capital of Egypt. The Ancient Egyptians seem to have recognized the importance of such central positions, as is clear from the names given to Memphis – *Ankh Tawy*, meaning "The Life of the Two Lands," and *Mkhat Tawy*, meaning "The Balance of the Two Lands."

Herodotus claimed that Menes, the first unifier of Egypt, had reclaimed from the Nile the ground on which he built The White Wall and its temple dedicated to the god Ptah.

It seems that before Memphis was built, the course of the Nile had to be changed, and there are two theories about this. The first is that the Nile's course at Memphis was static and that the city was reached by river by one or more lateral canals. Yet no traces of such canals were found to give credibility to this theory.

The second theory claimed by the team of the Egypt Exploration Society, when it carried out a survey of Memphis in 1982, is that "the river once flowed directly past the ruined field and has since receded eastwards by approximately 2.5 kilometers."

Whether Herodotus' story about the foundation of Memphis is true or not, there is no doubt that Menes created the town later known as Memphis. What we don't know is if Menes established it as a capital of the United Kingdom or just as a fortress to secure unity; nor do we know if it was Zoser, the first king of the 3rd dynasty, who took it as a capital. It remained the capital of Egypt during the Old Kingdom and was an important administrative and strategic city throughout the whole Pharaonic period, as re-flected in the splendor of the cemetery of Saqqara. Since Memphis was later known as *Hikuptah*, referring to the main god Ptah, and the Greeks may have taken the name "Aegyptos" from it, and extended the name of that important city to cover all of Egypt.

By the end of the Old Kingdom, Memphis suffered from political and social upheaval, and its importance decreased steadily, until the Hyksos were driven from the area at the end of the Second Intermediate Period. From the beginning of the New Kingdom until the end of Pharaonic history, Memphis was again one of the foremost cities in Egypt. It was the center of military activities, the main army base, and site of the military school and the manufacture of weapons and arms. It was also considered to be one of the royal residences, and many pharaohs built palaces there and constructed chapels that enlarged the area of the temple of the god Ptah. It was also the first and main city occupied by all the conquerors of Egypt in its late period – the Nubians, Assyrians, Persians and Macedonians.

The recent survey by the Egyptian Exploration Society led to a number of startling results, including the discovery of traces of the famous Memphis harbor.

The port of Memphis had been the chief center of shipbuilding, especially in the middle of the 18th dynasty. The ships built there were for military campaigns in Syro-Palestine. During Ptolemaic times, the port collected tax on all traffic passing through the city. Excavations revealed that Memphis was also a craftsmen's center, especially for carpentry and preparation of pigments.

Memphis maintained much of its importance even after the foundation of the city of Alexandria, which was chosen to be the capital of Egypt by Alexander the Great while he was on his way from Memphis to Siwa Oasis in about 330 B.C. With its splendid harbors, Alexandria became the greatest marketplace of the contemporary world and the most important city in the Hellenistic empire. Memphis, meanwhile, was finally deserted and entirely destroyed after the beginning of the Islamic era.

A small special museum houses the most important monument still preserved on the site: a magnificent colossus of Ramses II lying on its back. It is made out of one block of limestone and shows excellent workmanship. Its original height is estimated at about 45 feet, but it is now shorter, since a large part of the statue's legs, as well as one arm, are missing now. The royal cartouches are engraved on its shoulders, hand and girdle.

It is one of two huge colossi of Ramses II that adorned the main temple of Ptah. The second colossus has stood for more than 30 years in Ramses Square in the center of Cairo. It was brought from Memphis in 1954, when the Egyptian Government decided to erect in Cairo a colossal statue that would symbolize Ancient

Right: The upper part of the colossal limestone figure of Ramses II, representing the king in his youth, which now occupies its own museum in Memphis. Below: The right hand of the statue, inscribed with cartouches of Ramses II.

Egypt. The statue, more than 30 feet high, wears the double crown of Egypt. A third one was discovered in 1962 in very-bad condition, broken into three large pieces and about 40 smaller fragments. Early in 1986, in preparation for the exhibition of Ramses the Great in Memphis, Tennessee, in the United States, it was agreed that the colossus would be included. About 30 Egyptian restorers reassembled the colossus that now weighs 48 tons and is 28 feet high. The statue stands as the focal point of the exhibition of Ramses II, after passing thousands of years and crossing thousands of miles, as a testament to the power of international cultural relations.

Near the recumbent colossus in Memphis are scattered several statues and pieces of monuments, notably a fine alabaster sphinx, about 27 feet long, 13 feet high and weighing about 28 tons. Although it is uninscribed, its style suggests that it may belong to Amenophis III of the 18th dynasty.

Beside the ruins of the Great Temple of Ptah, which was excavated by the English archaeologist Flinders Petrie, are scattered fragments of monuments belonging to the New Kingdom and Late Periods. These include the palace of King Apries, from the 26th dynasty, and the embalming place of the Apis bull, which contains a fine alabaster embalming bed. Excavations and research are being conducted into King Siry I Chapel, the temple of Ramses II and the palace of King Merenptah, as well as other ruins that confirm the importance and vastness of the ancient city of Memphis.

The necropolis of Memphis extended more than 50 miles from Abu Roash on the north to Meidum on the south. Although most of the burials were in the two main cemeteries at Giza and Saqqara, the kings of the 5th dynasty usually built their pyramids and temple in Abu Sir and Abu Ghurab, nearly halfway between Giza and Saqqara. King Snefru, the founder of the 4th dynasty, built his two pyramids in Dahshur, a few miles south of Saqqara. Jedef Re, son of Cheops and the third king of the 4th dynasty, built his pyramid in Abu Roash, north of Giza, while Huny, the last king of the 3rd dynasty, built his pyramid at Meidum to the south of Dahshur.

Saqqara is an extensive stretch of land at the edge of the Western Desert, overlooking the city of Memphis. It occupies an area almost four miles long and not more than one mile wide. Its name possibly derives from Sokar (Sokaris in Greek), a hawk-headed god of the dead who dwelt in the desert west of Memphis. Another possibility is that the name is taken from a Bedouin tribe that lived in the area during the Middle Ages.

Saqqara cemetery includes tombs and architectural buildings ranging from the 1st dynasty to the Graeco-Roman Period, a span of more than 3,000 years. It is the largest cemetery in Egypt, housing about 20 pyramids and royal tombs, and hundreds of mastabas and private tombs, scattered around the Step Pyramid that dominates the site. (The mastaba is an Arabic word for the rectangular bench on which the Egyptian farmer used to sit with his friends in front of his house.) One of the richest archaeological sites in Egypt, it has frequently been explored and excavated over the past 140 years.

Excavations before World War II by Walter Emery led to the discovery of a group of large tombs – all plundered – belonging to the 1st dynasty. Some may have been actual tombs or even cenotaphs of kings, while others were built for the nobles and high-ranking officials.

Of all the monuments of Saqqara, none is more impressive or interesting than the Step Pyramid of Zoser, the founder of the 3rd dynasty. The pyramid marks an architectural evolution in the advanced planning and design of every element in the pyramid's complex. In its construction, nothing like it had been seen before and it is a true pioneer among the architectural miracles of antiquity.

The Step Pyramid complex reflects the impressive change from the mud-and-brick to rock-and-stone construction, and from the style of a simple flat rectangular mastaba to a design of a high, intricate pyramid with a complex of buildings. This striking development represents a great architectural evolution and a transition in belief concepts.

This enormous complex was constructed for King Zoser under the direction of his great architect Imhotep, who succeeded in building the first step pyramid anywhere on earth. His genius later became legendary and convinced people to come from every part of Egypt to Saqqara thousands of years after his death, making pilgrimages to his tomb, which the great archaeologist Emery had sought in vain. The Ancient Egyptians even made his name the third element in the Memphite triad in place of the god

Nefertum, composing the triad of Ptah with his wife Shmet and their son Imhotep. He was also identified by the Greeks with their god Aesculapius, god of medicine.

The Step Pyramid is a huge limestone structure, formed of six enormous *mastabas*, narrowing gradually on all four sides. The steps rise, like stairs to the sky, to a height of about 200 feet. The lowest "stage," a rectangle of 410 by 344 feet, anticipates Imhotep's development of the Egyptian tomb from a rectangular *mastaba* to a square pyramid.

The original entrance of the pyramid is at ground level on the north but another entrance was opened on the southern side during the 26th dynasty. However, because of the danger of falling blocks, it is forbidden to visit the inside through either entrance or to climb the pyramid. A large vertical shaft hewn in the subterranean rock beneath the pyramid leads to the burial chamber. It is surrounded by other chambers and corridors carved in the rock. Some of the elements are adorned with blue faience tiles imitating reed mats and with limestone reliefs representing Zoser performing religious ceremonies. More than 30,000 fine alabaster vases are stored inside the pyramid, but most of them were found to be broken.

The Step Pyramid is just one of the elements in Zoser's funerary complex, which is surrounded on every side by a rectangular limestone wall. The periphery of the wall extends for more than a mile at an approximate height of 33 feet and is decorated with recessed panels.

The entrance to the complex is located in the southeastern corner of the enclosure. It leads to a long colonnade composed of 40 columns in the shape of bundles of reeds. Each column is joined to the wall by another connecting wall.

Past the colonnade is the Heb Sed building. It consists of a court and an adjacent building in which Zoser might repeat in his second life the Jubilee ceremony, which the Egyptians called the Heb Sed. This ceremony was supposed to renew the king's strength. To the north of the Heb Sed are two large rectangular buildings, called the southern and northern houses. The facade of the southern one has lotus columns, representing the land of the south, while the northern building has papyri columns, representing the land of the north.

At the northern side of the Step Pyramid, in the middle of the complex court, is the Serdab, a very small building that remains virtually intact. It once contained a seated limestone statue of Zoser, which is now housed in Cairo Museum, while a copy has been put in the Serdab. To the west of the Serdab are the ruins of the mortal temple that is traditionally located to the north of a pyramid.

The complex also includes a tomb with underground rooms that resemble those of the pyramid. They have similar carved reliefs of the king and blue faience tiles on the walls. The function of this southern tomb – and of the southern and northern houses – is still under debate.

The Antiquities authorities have done an extensive job of restoring the subsidiary buildings of the complex, with the help of the French architect F. Lauer, who is still doing a job he began more than 60 years ago.

القَاهِرَة

In 1954, Zakaria Ghoneim discovered a huge unfinished pyramid to the southeast of Zoser's complex, belonging to Skhem Khet, the reputed successor of Zoser. This second Step Pyramid gained wide interest since it helped us to know more about the methods the Egyptians used to build their pyramids. Although none of the kings of the 3rd dynasty constructed a pyramid complex to compare with Zoser's it is clear that they had abandoned the *mastaba* style of tombs for this new style. An interesting example is the huge Step Pyramid constructed in Meidum, to the south of Saqqara, by Hwny, the last king of the 3rd dynasty.

Snefru, the first king of the 4th dynasty, built two pyramids in Dahshur, a short distance from Saqqara, from which they are visible because of their size and well-defined shape. Although the southern one was surely designed to be a true pyramid, with a square base and four sloping sides toward a point at the summit, its incline suddenly changes midway up the pyramid, a sure sign that the architects did not succeed in fulfilling their plans. Accordingly, this pyramid is called the bent, the rhomboidal, or the false pyramid. Its northern neighbor, which is larger and about 343 feet high, is considered the first true pyramid in Egypt.

During the 12th dynasty, 400 years later, kings Amenemhat II, Senusert II and Amenemhat III built their pyramid complexes in Dahshur to the east of Snefru's. They are smaller and not as well preserved.

In Saqqara, there is a limestone tomb in the form of a sarcophagus known as the *mastaba* of Pharaon. It was built by Shepseskaf, the sixth king of the 4th dynasty, on the western side

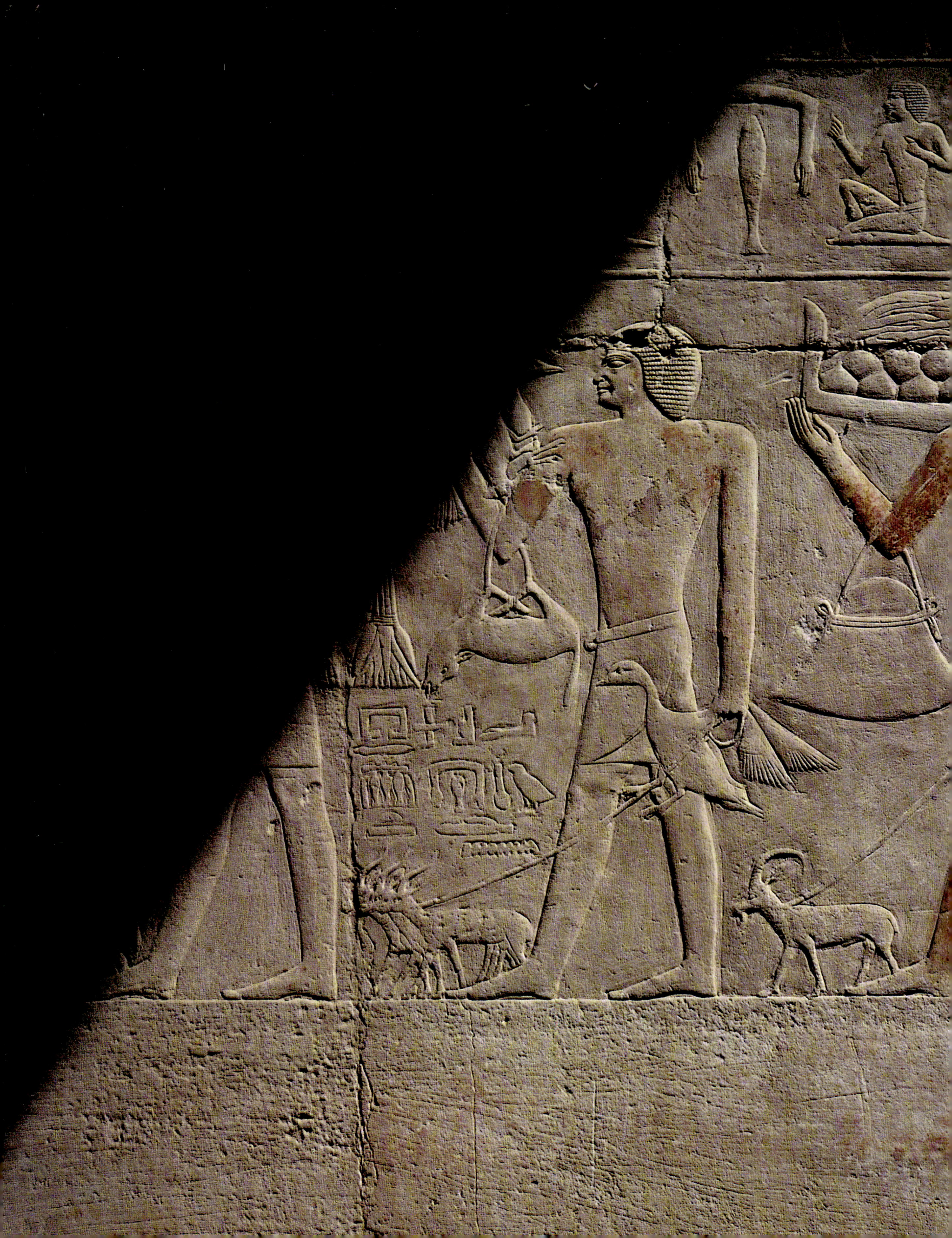

of the Saqqara plateau. It, like the tomb of his reputed sister Khentkaus at Giza, has gone back to the *mastaba* form.

In the 5th dynasty, the pharaohs chose a new burial place at Abu Sir and Abu Ghurab, halfway between Saqqara and Giza. Their pyramid complexes are distinguished by their rather high pyramids and uncovered sun temples, which were nicely decorated. Although they are in bad condition, they are still worth seeing. King User Kaf, the first king of the 5th dynasty, built his pyramid directly at the northeastern edge of Zoser's complex, but it is badly damaged because it was used as a quarry in the Late Period.

To the southwest of the Step Pyramid stands the Pyramid of Unas, the last king of the 5th dynasty. It is a small pyramid, about 55 feet high, whose core is composed of rubble and pieces of stones cased with limestone. Among several chambers in its interior is the funeral chamber with its granite sarcophagus still in place. It was the first pyramid ever decorated on the inside, and the walls of its chambers are covered with texts arranged in columns and painted in blue, called the Pyramid Texts. They are considered the oldest collection of religious and funerary texts, containing more than 750 spells to protect the deceased king. The ceilings are decorated with stars in imitation of the night sky. More than 1,000 years later, Prince Khamunese, son of Ramses II, inscribed on the bottom of the southern hall a record of his restorations on that pyramid. Similar inscriptions found in monuments at Abu Sir register his interest in preserving monuments of the Old Kingdom.

Most of the kings of the 6th dynasty – Teti, its founder; Pepi I; Merener; and Pepi II, the last king – built their pyramids in both northern and southern Saqqara. Some of them are decorated with the Pyramid Texts. Through the Saqqara tombs, belonging to kings from the 1st through the 6th dynasties, we can gain a clearer idea about the development of funeral and religious conceptions in the first 1,000 years of the Egyptian civilization.

Among the most interesting and celebrated monuments of Saqqara are the *mastabas* belonging to members of the royal family and high officials who were buried, usually with their families, in the vicinity of their kings. The *mastabas* were equipped with supporting pillars, false doors, offertory tables, statues and other amenities. They contain brilliant painted bas reliefs in a classical style from a period regarded as the golden age of Pharaonic art. The paintings symbolize activities, responsibilities and joys of the Egyptians' everyday lives: agricultural scenes, professions,

the feeding of animals, leisure-time amusements, fishing, and hunting for birds, hippopotami and crocodiles. Some of these scenes are full of charm, humor and other human feelings. Among a score of interesting tombs, the most famous of them is that of Moreruka (Mera), constructed for this important official, his wife and their son. It is the largest tomb and is composed of 31 rooms and passages. Other tombs, especially those of Ti, Ptah Hotep, Nefer, Kagemni Khnumhotep and Ankh Mahor, are also splendid. Among the later tombs of importance are those of General Horemheb, the last king of the 18th dynasty, and Tef Nakht from the 26th dynasty.

Mariette discovered in 1851 the serapeum to the northeast of the Step Pyramid, which contains the subterranean galleries where the sacred Apis bull was buried. Inside that rock-hewn sepulcher were found 24 granite and basalt sarcophagi, some of them weighing as much as 70 tons. The bull Apis was worshiped in Memphis and was associated with the main god Ptah.

Nearby is an open space that was adorned in the Ptolemaic period with statues of Greek philosophers. The ruins of a Coptic monastery lie at the edge of the desert to the southeast of the Step Pyramid. It is the monastery of St. Germeah, dating from the 5th century A.D.

القـاهــرة

Of all Egypt's heritage, the deepest impressions and greatest admiration are reserved for those three massive triangular-faced monuments, which the Greeks called "The Pyramids," and for that huge leonine statue with a human face, which they called "The Sphinx." All four rise from an expanse of sand on the Giza Plateau.

No doubt those three pyramids and the great Sphinx are the most famous, glorious and renowned of all Egyptian monuments. Giza, which began as a medieval town to the west of Cairo, is now a large modern city and an important part of Metropolitan Cairo, but its fame is linked with its magnificent monuments.

The three pyramids at Giza are arranged from northeast to southwest in chronological order and in a descending volume, size and standard of perfection. Their owners – Cheops (Khufu), his son Khefren (Khafra) and his grandson Mycerinus (Menkaure) – represent three successive generations of the 4th Pharaonic dynasty. Those pyramids were built mostly of local limestone, condition, 139 feet long and weighing about 15 tons. It is considered the oldest "big ship" ever discovered. The boat now stands in a magnificent museum in the form of a ship, located on the top of the pit that housed the dismantled parts of the boat. The second pit, neighbouring the first one on the west, has not yet been opened.

Egyptian records shed no light on the construction of the three pyramids at Giza. Herodotus, the father of history, reported that 100,000 men shared in the task of building the Great Pyramid, working three months every year during flood time for 20 years. Even so, the debate continues over the method of building the pyramids. It is clear, however, that the stones were raised from ground level by means of artificial ramps — as determined by the fact that the remains of such ramps have been discovered in the pyramid sites of El Lisht, Meidum and Amon Temple at Karnak. Before being raised up, the blocks of stone must have been dragged by human hands and carried on sleds drawn by oxen.

The Great Pyramid is amazing for the genius of its planning, its survival over the past 5,000 years with very little damage, and its inner design. Equally amazing is the volume of the task and the perfect administration needed to raise the pyramid, its complex and the pyramid city, using the simplest implements and elementary technology available during Cheops' reign of no more than 25 years. The architects showed great cleverness in choosing the most appropriate site in the desert to bear 2.3 million blocks of stone — a site near the Nile and not far from local quarries. What is also astonishing was their ability to level the site and flatten a surface of 13 acres to an equal level, differing by no more than half an inch from one corner to another; their ability to orient the four sides of the pyramid to the four cardinal points; and their capacity in casing the enormous surfaces of the pyramid with the limestone from Tura and pink granite from Aswan.

Not surprisingly, many attempts have been made to prove that Cheops' Pyramid was not only a burial place, and many reasons have been given for building such a mountain of stone. Nor is it surprising that a number of books dealing with the secrets and hidden powers of that pyramid have been written in recent years. There is, however, no evidence to support such ideas and suppositions. At the same time, many scientists became

interested in solving the mysteries of the pyramids through modern science and technology. Cosmic rays and geophysical methods were used to discover the inside of the second pyramid, but they did not succeed in adding to our knowledge. Investigations using microgravimetric readings and electromagnetic soundings are now being conducted in the Great Pyramid under the auspices of the Egyptian Antiquities Department. We hope that these tests will help us to know more about the Cheops Pyramid and to reveal some of its secrets.

Of all the pharaohs who followed Cheops, only his son Khefren dared to build a pyramid and its complex competing in volume, magnitude and perfection with that of his father.

The Pyramid of Khefren, the second of the Giza group, is situated on the southwest side of Cheops' Pyramid. It gives the impression of being taller than Cheops, because it is built on slightly higher ground, but in reality it is eight feet shorter than the Great Pyramid. Most of its casing has disappeared, but a granite casing can still be seen on its summit. It has two entrances facing the north, one about 50 feet high and another below it.

The funerary temple of Khefren's Pyramid is virtually destroyed, while the causeway has disappeared except for the portion near the Valley Temple, which is built of granite and thus is called the Granite Temple. It stands near the Sphinx and attracts the eye with its simplicity and perfection. Flanking the funerary temple are what appear to be six boat pits, but no boats were found in them.

The third pyramid of Giza, built by Mycerinus, occupies less than half of the area covered by the Great Pyramid, and is only about 230 feet high. Its lower 16 courses are still cased in granite. The mortuary temple lies to the east of the pyramid, which is fronted on its southern side by three subsidiary pyramids for the queens, each not more than 30 feet high. All three are badly damaged. Khent Kaus, the last queen of the 4th dynasty, built her *mastaba* in the shape of a sarcophagus, beside the third pyramid. Many *mastabas* and rock-cut tombs are spread over the area. Their walls are covered with scenes from everyday life and drawings of the deceased and his family. They include the well-known tomb of Queen Meres Ankh III, wife of Khefren; the tomb of Kar, overseer of the pyramids; and the *mastaba* of Idu, a high priest.

In the early evening, after sunset, the pyramids of Giza come to life through the spectacle of sound and light. The colored floodlights, the playful shadows, the attractive narration and the fitting music give the monuments new dimensions.

Left: The Solar Boat of Cheops, discovered beside the Great Pyramid in 1954 and reassembled 15 years later, now on display in its own museum. Below: Details of a relief from the tomb of Kagemni at Saqqara.

but also contain fine limestone from Tura and Aswan, as well as granite. The use of granite must have caused serious problems owing to its hardness, heaviness and need to be transported from Aswan quarries more than 500 miles from Giza.

Egyptian civilization was nearly 3,000 years old when Greek travelers like Herodotus visited Egypt and saw the huge pyramids standing on the edge of the desert and looking toward the River Nile. It was a sight unlike any ever seen or dreamt of in Greece. When Napoleon made his military expedition to Egypt, he calculated that the stones of the Giza pyramids would have been sufficient to build a wall 10 feet high and one foot wide, running around the whole of France. It has been calculated that the volume of the Great Pyramid could house London's Westminster Abbey, Paris' Notre Dame Cathedral and Rome's St. Peter Cathedral altogether. It has also been said that if the 2.3 million stones of the Great Pyramid were cut in smaller pieces, they might be used to build a city for 100,000 inhabitants. Yet another speculation is that if the stones of the Great Pyramid were divided into one foot cubes and extended in a straight line, they would reach two-thirds of the way around the Equator.

The site of the Giza necropolis is certainly one of the best preserved, excavated, registered and studied of all pyramid sites, and it has had a vital role in clarifying the different aspects of royal funerary establishments of the Old Kingdom. Nevertheless, there are still some isolated areas that ought to be excavated, and a great deal of significant research that is still needed to provide us with important new scientific data.

The largest and oldest of the three is the Great Pyramid of Cheops, built about 4,500 years ago; it is one of the seven wonders of antiquity, and a monument that made the name of Cheops famous all over the world. Its base covers an area of 13 hectares, its original height was 481 feet before it lost its summit (which was about 31 feet high), and it is estimated to contain 2.3 million limestone blocks averaging 2.5 tons, although some stones may weigh as much as 15 tons.

The original entrance in the northern face of the pyramid is 55 feet above the ground. Since it is blocked, the pyramid is now entered through a hole that was made during the 9th century in the false hope of finding treasures hidden inside.

The monument's interior is almost as impressive as its exterior. Here are corridors, passageways, rooms, apertures for ventilation; here too is a grand gallery, 153 feet long and 28 feet high with a braced ceiling and a burial room, called "the King's Room," with a ceiling of nine blocks of granite weighing about 400 tons, supported by five pillars to reduce the pressure on the ceiling. It is not only an extraordinary work, but a miracle seemingly beyond human capacity at such a remote time.

We now believe that Cheops originally planned a smaller tomb with an underground burial chamber, but it was not completed. As his ambitions for it grew, he altered the tomb's plan twice, each time deciding to raise the burial chamber higher and to increase the size of his pyramid. His second project needed an upward sloping corridor, and another smaller horizontal one leading to the burial room, which was later mistakenly called "the Queen's Room." The third project called for enlarging and extending the main corridor, which is now called "the Grand Gallery" and leads to the new burial room (the King's Chamber), where the lidless granite sarcophagus of the king is still housed.

To the east of the pyramid lie the ruins of the funerary temple, which was a rectangular building of limestone connected by a long causeway to a second lower temple, the Valley Temple, on the edge of the desert. It is presently covered by the houses of the village of Nazlet El Seman. Three small pyramids, now in bad condition, are the tombs of his queens and are situated to the east of the pyramid. Rows of stone *mastabas*, running parallel on the western and southern sides, belonged to nobles, high priests and members of the royal family during that period.

More than 60 years ago, the American archaeologist Reisner excavated three huge pits in the shape of big boats on the east side of the pyramid, but he found nothing inside those pits and his work was unrewarded. But in 1954, Kamal El Malakh, chief architect of Giza, was working on the southeastern side of Cheops' Pyramid when he discovered two pits covered with 41 limestone slabs. After opening the eastern pit, which was 103 feet long and 17 feet deep, he found at its bottom 1,224 wooden pieces. These pieces, mostly of Lebanese cedar, ranged in length between 75 feet and less than four inches and were arranged in 13 orderly layers. It clearly constituted the largest archaeological boat ever discovered, and it became known as the Solar Barque of Cheops. This discovery added to Cheops' fame, and raised questions in scientific circles about its construction, dismantling, burial, and religious and funeral significance.

The wooden pieces were fitted, restored, chemically treated, assembled and bound with their old cords by restorer Haj Ahmed Yousef, in a difficult, complicated and long operation that lasted for 15 years. The result was a gigantic boat, almost in perfect

Southeast of the Great Pyramid, near the village of Nazlet El Seman, lies a gigantic Sphinx (called in Arabic *Abou El Hawl*). It has the body of a lion and a human head and face, and is believed to be the portrait of Khefren. Most likely, when the architects and sculptors were preparing the causeway of Khefren's complex, they came to a knoll. Instead of flattening it, they transformed it into a Sphinx. Later in the New Kingdom, they identified the statue with the Sun God Hor-m-akhty. The Sphinx is 240 feet long and 66 feet high, and faces the east, probably to greet the rising sun.

A great granite stela, found beneath the sand in 1916 and lying between the paws of the Sphinx, was erected by King Thutmoses IV (18th dynasty), 1,000 years after the Sphinx was sculpted. The inscription on the stela relates that when Thutmoses was a prince, he went hunting in the desert near the pyramids. Becoming tired, he lay down to have a nap in the shade of the Sphinx. While he was sleeping, he dreamt that the Sun God promised him that if he removed the sand around the monument, he would be entitled to ascend the Egyptian throne.

The Giza Sphinx is not only the oldest one in Egypt, but also the largest and most mysterious of all the sphinxes. Beyond it stands a limestone temple that is related to it and is called the "Sphinx Temple."

According to legend from Middle Ages, an emir who hated the Sphinx's pagan smile destroyed its nose and mouth with his cannon. Another story is that this destruction was caused by Napoleon's cannons in the Pyramids Battle with the Mamelukes. I believe that decay is the real cause of this destruction, since the Sphinx is sculpted in soft limestone, and has suffered considerably from erosion and from the rising of the underground water table.

القـاهـرة

Although more than 80 Egyptian pyramids still survive in Egypt and Sudan, most of them are little more than mounds of loose stone and sand. The most important and well-known ones are from the Pyramid Age (the Old Kingdom). All were built on the edge of the Western Desert, from Abu Roash in the north to Meidum in the South, in what we can call the Necropolis of Memphis, the capital during that period.

القـاهـرة

Today, the grand city of Cairo, with its museum, its transferred obelisks and statues, the Heliopolis ruins, as well as Memphis and Saqqara, symbolizes and represents Pharaonic Egypt and its remote civilization, although the actual city was established 10 centuries ago – nearly 14 centuries after the disappearance of the pharaohs.

THE COPTIC LEGACY *Dr. Gawdat Gabra*

Our knowledge about Egypt during the Roman, Byzantine and early Islamic periods is based mainly on the written material preserved on papyri, parchment and ostraca (potsherds or stone chips bearing inscriptions). Many Greek, Roman and Arabic historians left detailed reports covering all aspects of life in Egypt.

When Octavius, later Emperor Augustus, defeated Antonius in the sea battle of Actium in 31 B.C., he was able to occupy Alexandria and to put an end to the Ptolemaic dynasty in Egypt under its famous queen Cleopatra. Egypt became a Roman province under the personal authority of the emperor. The new rulers had to introduce different administrative and agricultural reforms to stop the instability that had prevailed in the last decade of the Ptolemaic period. Egypt was for Rome the most important supplier of corn. In addition to transporting corn to Rome, Egyptians were subjected to other forms of forced labor. At the same time, they faced a heavy burden from the poll tax and other taxes.

In order to defend the country and to crush any rebellion, the Romans placed legions at Pelusium to control the eastern Delta, at Alexandria to control the western Delta, and at Babylon to control the rest of Egypt. Emperors presented themselves as pharaohs and erected Egyptian-style temples in honor of Egyptian gods. The Greeks, though no longer rulers, remained among the elite of society, especially in the self-governing cities. The Greek language continued to be the official language, while Latin was used mainly in the army. The Egyptians kept their own ancient language, as seen on the walls of the temples and especially in the demotic and Coptic writings.

During the Roman occupation of Egypt, resistance sometimes flared up, especially among the people of Thebes. In 172 A.D., in the Delta there was even an uprising of herdsmen. The Roman army also had to interfere to stop fights between Greeks and Jews, especially in Alexandria. The Blemmyes, a Nubian tribe, often attacked Upper Egypt and threatened the flow of commerce between the Red Sea and the Nile Valley. Meanwhile, severe economic conditions throughout Egypt prompted the Emperor Diocletian to introduce administrative reforms in 297.

At the same time, Alexandria developed into one of the most important and cosmopolitan cities of the civilized world and its population represented different currents of cultures, religions and philosophies. There, and elsewhere in Egypt, feelings of nationalism increased among the oppressed people. A catalyst for these feelings was the spread of Christianity in the area.

The Christians became subjected to such persecution under Diocletian that the Coptic church begins its calendar with the Era of Diocletian, known also as the Era of the Martyrs. The official persecution of Christians by the Romans finally ceased between the years 311 and 313 through the Edict of Toleration and the Edict of Milan.

The final years of the Byzantine rule of Egypt were characterized by large estates. Strong land-owning families even usurped governmental functions. Under this feudal system, most native Egyptians were relegated to serfdom.

In the first decades of the 7th century the Persian army attacked Syria and Egypt. Despite the efforts of Emperor Heraclius, Egypt was soon lost to the Byzantine Empire. The emergence of Islam brought a new power to the Arabian Peninsula. In 643 the Arabian army general Amr Ibn el-As extended the complete authority of the Islamic state of Egypt. A new era began in the long history of this country.

القاهرة

The Coptic Church is one of the oldest in the world. According to tradition, it was founded by St. Mark the Evangelist. We are told that he preached the Gospel in Alexandria as early as 50 or 60 A.D. Gradually Christianity began to spread in the Nile Valley — as evidenced by the appointment of several Egyptian bishops by Demetrius, the Patriarch of Alexandria (188–230). The Catechetical school of Alexandria was the most important theological school of the time, led by great scholars of the 2nd and 3rd centuries such as Pantaenus, Clement and Origen.

The Egyptian Christians were first persecuted in the year 201 during the reign of the Emperor Septimius Severus. The Copts suffered another persecution during the reign of Decus (249–251). Each citizen had to prove that he made offerings to the gods. Thousands of Egyptians preferred death rather than to deny their Christian faith. Many escaped into the desert and others were captured and tortured. The most severe wave of persecution began during the reign of the Emperor Diocletian (284–305) and continued under Maximinus Daia (305–313). Church sources speak of hundreds of thousands of martyrs enduring a long, systematic persecution. The Patriarch Peter I was described as the "Seal of the Martyrs." The commemoration of martyrs as saints is an important feature of the Coptic church.

The Patriarchs of Alexandria played a remarkable role in religious policy and had a leading position in universal theological controversies, especially in the 4th and 5th centuries. The Patriarch Alexander and his young deacon Athanasius, later the most distinguished Patriarch of Alexandria, fought against the heresy of Arius, who was condemned during the Council of Nicaea in 325. The Creed of Faith, which survives to this day, was a result of that Council. It is said that 318 bishops from around the civilized world assembled there.

With the career of Patriarch Athanasius (328–373), who was exiled five times by the Roman authorities as a hero of orthodoxy and defender of the faith, national feeling increased among the Egyptians. Athanasius' struggles and exiles were a glorious part of the history of the Coptic Church and a spur to Egyptian nationalism.

The "unity or duality of Christ" was a matter of controversy among theologians for many years. An irresolvable schism resulted in the church after the Council of Chalcedon (451). At the same time, the Coptic Church became a national church, united behind the Patriarch of Alexandria.

The emperors of the Byzantine Empire wanted to fill the see of Alexandria with men loyal to Constantinople who would provide them with imperial political and military support. The Copts recognized only their patriarch, who often had to leave Alexandria to lead his church far from the Byzantine authorities. In 631 Emperor Heraclius sent Cyrus – known also as al-Muqauqas – to Alexandria as an imperial prefect to control Egypt and to continue as a loyal patriarch to the Empire. Cyrus forced the Patriarch Benjamin to flee from Alexandria to Upper Egypt in the years 631–644, and even attacked monasteries to hunt out the heads of the Coptic Church.

The last ten years of the Byzantine rule in Egypt were among the fullest in Egyptian history.

The Arab conquest of Egypt, which put an end to Byzantine rule there, had immeasurable consequences for the history of the Coptic Church. It is a wonder that the Church survived the many waves of persecution. Still, it had a direct influence on other churches in Africa. Cyrenaica, the Pentapolis of the five towns (between Tripolis and Alexandria), appear to this day in the title of the Coptic Patriarch. The Nubian Church was also influenced by the Coptic Church. We know that a bishop was in Philae as early as 362 A.D. Recent excavations in Nubia show the good relations between the two churches continuing as late as the time of Patriarch Gabriel IV (1370–8) who consecrated a bishop for the people of Nubia. For many centuries the Coptic Patriarchs sent a monk from Egypt to be the head of the Ethiopian Church. This tradition remained in effect from the 4th century until 1948.

القَاهِرَة

Monasticism is, perhaps, the Copts' most important contribution to civilization. It had a special character in Egypt where one could stand with one foot on fertile agricultural land and the other on the desert. During the Decian persecution (251 A.D.) many Christians fled into the desert, and some discovered that life there was more suitable for religious practice and meditation.

We know nothing of the first monks other than the absence of rules by which they had to live. We do know, however, about St. Antony, considered to be the father of monasticism. Antony was born around the year 251 and died when he was 105 years old after living 70 years as an anchorite. Patriarch Athanasius the Great compiled the biography of that eminent hermit, which was soon known in Europe.

In about 320, St. Pachom established the first community of monks at Tabennisi, in the district of Nag' Hammadi, in Upper Egypt. His form of monasticism, known as cenobitic, was based on precise rules. These rules cover all aspects of monastic life such as prayers, masses, calls, meals and work. Cenobitic monasticism proved highly popular, and monasteries spread throughout the country, especially in Middle and Upper Egypt. Many fathers of the Church from different parts of the world desired to learn about monasticism and spent time in Egypt, especially in the 4th and 5th centuries; they included St. John Chrysostom, bishop of Constantinople; Rufinus, the ecclesiastical historian; and St. Basil, the author of the liturgy. The monastic rules of Pachom were translated from Coptic into Latin and this directly influenced monasticism in Europe.

Another great figure of monasticism is Shenoute, who accompanied the Patriarch Cyril to the Council of Ephesus in 431. His monastery, known as Deir al-Abiad, or the White Monastery, received thousands of refugees in hard times. Shenoute was also a great preacher, administrator and nationalist who struggled against heathenism and Hellenism.

Left: A remnant of the Babylon Fortress, an interesting example of Roman and Byzantine military construction. Below: A fresco in a niche from Bawit (7th century). The lower part represents the Holy Virgin Mary with the Christ Child and apostles. The upper part represents God in the Chariot of Fire with the four symbolic creatures.

Following pages: Two views of the Church of the Holy Virgin Mary, called the "Suspended" or "Hanging" church because it was built on the ruins of the Babylon Fortress.

Left: A section of the wooden door from the Church of St. Barbara; 4th/5th century, now in the Coptic Museum. Below: The famous sycamore tree of the Holy Virgin Mary in the suburb of al-Matarya.

To the west of the Delta (*Wadi al-Natrun*) many colonies of monks were founded in the desert during the 4th century. Literary sources inform us about the hermits in Scetis and about the famous Macarius, the founder of monasticism in this district. Hundreds of monks' cells with interesting architecture and fine wall paintings have recently been discovered in Kellia. The earliest date back to the 4th/5th centuries.

The monks played a considerable role throughout the history of the Coptic Church. The great Athanasius was the first Patriarch who encouraged monks to become bishops. Since the 8th century most of the patriarchs of the Alexandria see have been elected from the monasteries in Wadi al-Natrun. The Coptic monasteries received Greeks, Romans, Nubians, Ethiopians, Syrians, Libyans and others.

القَـاهِـرَة

Cairo can be proud of its Coptic legacy. The most significant group of Christian monuments lies within the Roman and Byzantine Fortress of Babylon with its ancient churches and the Coptic Museum. Another group is to be seen in old Cairo outside the Babylon Fortress. A third group is represented by some important churches scattered about different parts of Cairo. Some monuments are associated with the flight of the Holy Family.

The Fortress of Babylon lies on the east bank of the River Nile in the district known today as Old Cairo. The site has been a bishop's residence since the middle of the 5th century or earlier. The Fortress dates from early Roman times, when a Roman legion resided in this strategic point between Upper and Lower Egypt. Apparently it was enlarged and fortified by the emperors Trajan (98–117 A.D.) and Arcadius (395–408). The Coptic historian John of Nikou tells us that the Arabs were able to spread their authority over Egypt after holding this well-fortified fortress. The Babylon Fortress had 10 bastions, of which four are partly preserved. One of its two towers and the southern gateway can be seen from the gardens of the Coptic Museum. Most of the walls are built of three regular layers of red bricks alternating with five stone layers. The remains of this fortress provide an interesting example of Roman and Byzantine military buildings.

The ancient churches within the Fortress of Babylon – known also as *Qasr el-Sham* – are almost certainly the oldest in Cairo.

Pieces of woodwork dating from the 4th and 5th centuries were found in the churches of al-Mo-allaqa, St. Barbara and St. Sergius. These masterpieces are now displayed in the Coptic Museum. While it seems incongruous that these churches existed inside a Roman and Byzantine military fortress, it is not unlikely that the churches were built sometime after the end of the persecution of the Christians.

The Church of the Holy Virgin Mary (*al-Mo-allaqa*) is called the "Suspended" or "Hanging" Church because it was erected upon the ruins of two southern bastions of the Babylon Fortress. Its famous wooden lintel with the scene of Christ's entry into Jerusalem, now in the Coptic Museum, dates to the 4th/5th centuries. The church was partly demolished in the time of the Patriarch Joseph (831–850) and was rebuilt by the Patriarch Abraham (976–979). When the patriarchal seat of Alexandria was transferred to Cairo in the 11th century, it was located in Mo-allaqa in view of the church's importance.

In 1672 the Frenchman Venselb referred to Mo-allaqa as the most ancient and beautiful church in Egypt. This church, like many ancient churches of Egypt, is of a basilican type adopted from ancient Egyptian temples. It has a front vestibule or a narthex leading to the main church with its nave, columns, ambos and sanctuaries. The columns that separate the aisles are executed in marble, except for one that is of black basalt. Some of the capitals of these columns are Corinthian, presumably taken from older Graeco-Roman buildings. The attractive ambo or pulpit is attributed to the 13th century. It rests upon 15 marble pillars inlaid with mosaics. In the eastern part of the church stand three sanctuaries. The one in the center is dedicated to the Holy Virgin, the right-hand one to John the Baptist, and the left-hand one to St. George. The splendid screen or iconostasis of the middle sanctuary dates to the 12th/13th centuries and is of ebony inlaid with ivory. The altar inside the sanctuary is surmounted by a canopy and supported by four columns. Behind the altar is a marble tribune, where the clergy usually sat. As in many Coptic churches, the Church of Mo-allaqa is decorated by very interesting icons.

A small door of fine pine wood in the southern aisle of the main church leads into the "little church." This church was built on the floor of one of the bastions of the Fortress. To the left is the sanctuary of Teckle Haimanout, the famous saint of Ethiopia. Traces of fine wall paintings are still visible on its eastern wall. One of the scenes, in what is most likely the oldest preserved part of the church, apparently represents Jesus Christ flanked by Apostles. Coptic frescoes have recently been discovered there, showing a wonderful scene of the Nativity.

To the south of the sanctuary is the baptistery, which contains a granite basin and a niche ornamented with mosaics. Although this church has been restored at several different times – most recently in 1983 – it still preserves the atmosphere of a medieval Coptic church.

The Church of Saints Sergius and Bacchus (*Abu-Sarga*) can be reached through a door in the garden of the Coptic Museum. It is probably the oldest church in Cairo, having been built over a traditional site blessed by the Holy Family. The Church of Abu-Sarga also has historical importance. The 55th Patriarch, Shenoute I (858–869), was the first to be consecrated in this church. After him, patriarchs of the Coptic Church continued to be elected there up to the beginning of the 12th century.

The church is of a basilican type. Its front vestibule or narthex has a Mandatum Tank that was used for the service of the blessing of water on the Feast of Epiphany, though today a portable basin is used. Two rows of six columns each separate the aisles from the church's nave. Eleven of these monolithic columns are of marble, and one is of red granite. The columns still preserve traces of painted figures, which appear to represent apostles or saints. Some panels of the old wooden church's pulpit are in the Coptic Museum; others are in the British Museum. The pulpit has been replaced by a copy of the marble ambo of the Church of St. Barbara, which is nearby. The screen or iconostasis of the main sanctuary is a wonderful piece of art. It is attributed to the 12th/13th centuries. Its fine panels are inlaid with ivory and ebony, carved in a very attractive relief with arabesques. Some wooden panels are of special importance, being of older origin. They represent three warrior saints, the Nativity and the Last Supper. The altar stands inside the sanctuary, surmounted by a lofty canopy supported by four pillars. A semi-circular tribune with seven steps was built around the walls of the apse. It is decorated with strips of red, black and white marble. The bishop's throne with the niche that lies behind it is in the center of the apse. The icons of the Church of Abu-Sarga are of special interest. Some of them are relatively old and could be assigned to the 16th/17th centuries. They represent the life history of Christ, the Holy Virgin and some of the Saints.

The Church of Abu-Sarga also boasts the Crypt of the Chapel of the Holy Family.

Many other Coptic monuments were erected in the same enclosure of the Roman and Byzantine Fortress of Babylon. Although they are not famous like the churches of al-Mo-allaqa and Abu-Sarga, they show the great importance of this site for the patriarchs of the Coptic Church. These are the Church of St. Barbara, the Church of St. George, the Church of the Virgin known as *Qasriat al-Rihan*, and the convent of the nuns of St. George. It is noteworthy that a Jewish synagogue is also located in the enclosure.

القَـاهِـرَة

The Coptic Museum is the one institution in Cairo that best conveys the Coptic legacy. Its status as a monument reflects its unique position within the Fortress of Babylon, surrounded by Cairo's oldest churches, as well as its attractive *mashrabias*, windows, wooden arabesque ceilings and arches.

Marcus Simaika founded the museum in 1908, but portions of it are actually much older. Some *mashrabias* and parts of the ceilings were brought to the museum from other older buildings. In 1931 the museum was put under government control and a new wing was subsequently established in 1947.

With its 14,000 pieces, the Coptic Museum boasts the largest collection of Coptic art in the world. A significant number of the exhibited objects originate from Cairo and its environs, such as Saqqara and Memphis. Many fine pieces – such as wooden panels and doors, icons, metal censers and bible caskets, pottery, sculptures and manuscripts – once belonged to edifices within the Babylon Fortress.

In 1983 the greater part of the museum was renovated and the objects were displayed according to material, consistent with modern methods of exhibition. Most of the exhibited monuments go back to the periods between the 3rd and 13th centuries. The abundance of precious objects demonstrates the development of Coptic art as a popular, individual and national art. These monuments represent the different aspects of Coptic civilization.

The section of woodwork in the old wing contains carved and painted panels, friezes, doors, combs and musical instruments that reflect the skill of Coptic carpenters. A special section is dedicated to Coptic pottery, which is famous for its different techniques, variety of forms, fine designs and decoration in lovely colors.

Below: A bronze lamp representing the cross amid the crescent; 14th/15th century, Coptic Museum. Right: A 15th-century silver casket for the Gospel; from the Church of Abu-Sarga, now in the Coptic Museum.

On the first floor of the new wing is exhibited the collection of Coptic stonework, the most important of which are the architectural carvings: niches, columns, capitals, lintels and friezes. They illustrate the development of Coptic sculpture. The masterpieces of stonework of such high quality bear witness to the splendid churches and monasteries that once existed in Egypt.

Textiles are the most characteristic products of Coptic art. Coptic textiles were exported all over the world during Roman, Byzantine and Islamic times. The Coptic Museum possesses a rich collection of textiles. The collection is on the upper floor of the new wing and contains tunics, curtains, parts of shrouds and various fragments.

On the same floor are the icons, metalwork and manuscripts. Most of the icons were brought from Cairo's old churches. Although the bulk of them are not more than three centuries old, they are very interesting for their themes. Some of them bear features of old Coptic art. The names of some artists are immortalized on icons. The metalwork section is remarkable for its different materials such as gold, silver, copper, bronze and iron. It contains objects from everyday life: jewels, medical instruments, keys and lamps. Many churches' liturgical vessels, crosses and Bible caskets reflect the skill of Coptic craftsmen. Of great importance is the museum's collection of manuscripts on papyrus, parchment and paper. The texts are written in Old Greek, Coptic, Syriac, Arabic and Ethiopian. Coptic Gnostic codices could be considered one of the most valuable collections of papyri in the world. Both wings of the museum also contain wonderful frescoes. These masterpieces tell us how the monasteries and churches once were decorated.

The Coptic Museum also possesses fine collections of glass, ivory and ostraca.

القَهِرَة

Old Cairo boasts of more Christian monuments than any other district of the city. To the south of the Fortress lie some minor churches. The Church of the Holy Virgin belongs to a small convent of Babylon known as the Cloister of Babylon al-Darag. In the same spot stands the convent of Theodore with the Church of Saints Cyrus and John and the Church of Theodore the Eastern. To the north of the Fortress lies an important group of churches,

not far from the mosque of Amr at Al-Fustat. These are the Church of Mercurius (*Abu-Saifain*), the Church of Shenoute (*Shenouda*), and the Church of the Virgin Mary, known as al-Damshiria. A nunnery is also located there. North of Al-Fustat are the Church of St. Minas (*Mena*) and the Church of St. Behnam at Fom al-Khalig.

This group of churches provide evidence of the expansion of Christian buildings north of the Babylon Fortress and of Al-Fustat long before the foundation of Fatimid Cairo. So we know, for example, that the Patriarch Michael I was elected in the Church of Shenoute in the year 743 A.D. The famous historian Al-Maqreezi tells us that the Church of St. Minas in Fom al-Khalig was restored in 724 A.D.

The most significant church of this group is St. Mercurius. According to tradition, this church was restored around 927 A.D. – and in the year 1080, 47 bishops assembled there. The nave of the church is separated from its narthex or front vestibule by a screen. Its beautiful ambo is decorated with mosaics and is supported by 15 marble columns. The central sanctuary of the church is dedicated to St. Mercurius. Its screen is a wonderful piece of art of ebony inlaid with fine engraved plaques of ivory. The doorway is flanked with two Corinthian columns of marble.

The church is famous for its interesting icons. Over the doorway of the screen or iconostasis are two icons, one of Christ, the other of the Holy Virgin Mary. The lower row has icons of Christ in the center; the Holy Virgin, the Archangel Michael and three apostles on His right; and St. John the Baptist, the Archangel Gabriel and three apostles on His left. The church's sanctuary is imposing. Its altar is surmounted by an attractive canopy decorated with wonderful paintings. The most important scene shows Christ surrounded by the Four Creatures, symbolizing the four Evangelists, and by the seraphim. A fine tribune of red and white marble is behind the altar. The east wall of the niche has frescoes with Christ and the seraphim; the walls around are ornamented with paintings representing the 12 apostles.

Many historians, among them al-Maqreezi and Abu Saleh, have stated that Fatimid Cairo and its later extensions had many old churches. But most were destroyed in times of disorder and anarchy, especially during the reign of the Mameluke Sultan el-Naser Mohammad Ibn Qalawoon. Of those that still exist, the churches of Haret al-Rum and Haret Zuwaila are considered among the most important.

The Church of the Holy Virgin Mary at Haret al-Rum is

situated in the quarter of al-Ghoria. It was probably founded in the 10th century and was restored in 1086. It was a patriarchal seat during the years 1660–1799. In the years 1460, 1703 and 1785 Holy Chrism was consecrated there. The church has a narthex, nave and three sanctuaries. Five piers separate its choir from the nave. Seven icons adorn the wooden pulpit of the church, representing Christ, the four Evangelists, St. John Chrysostom and St. George. The iconostasis of the central sanctuary is in wood inlaid with ivory. Its top is decorated by an icon of the Holy Virgin flanked on each side by six icons of apostles. The ceiling of the church consists of 120 domes, three of which are over its three sanctuaries. A little church of St. Theodore with one sanctuary and a baptistery is attached to its northern aisle. In the upper floor of the Church of the Holy Virgin is the Church of St. George. The same group also includes the convent of nuns of St. Theodore.

Another important complex of Coptic monuments is to be found in Haret Zuwaila, near al-Muski in the district known as al-Khurinfish. We are told that the Holy Family blessed the place. This complex includes the Church of the Holy Virgin, the Church of Mercurius (*Abu-Saifain*) and the Church of St. George. A convent of nuns is attached to the Church of the Holy Virgin. The oldest of the three, the Church of the Holy Virgin was probably founded in the 10th/11th century and later, for three centuries – until the year 1660 – was a patriarchal seat. The church has a narthex, nave, choir, two aisles and three sanctuaries. Most of the church's marble columns have Corinthian capitals. Of special attraction is the screen before the sanctuaries, the dome of the altar in the central sanctuary and the tribune in its apse. The church contains many interesting icons, including one that represents the Annunciation and dates from 1355 A.D.

The district of Abbasia, where the new Cathedral stands, is known for its attractive, but relatively new churches. One of them, the Church of Anba Ruwais, was mentioned by al-Maqreezi. The most important part of this church is the crypt where Anba Ruwais is buried, as are some patriarchs of the 14th and 15th centuries. The Patriarch Marcus VIII (1796–1809) transferred his seat from Haret al-Rum to the district of al-Esbakia. A church was erected there around the year 1800. The church was rebuilt into a cathedral during the 19th century and is known as the Cathedral of St. Mark, though its style resembles that of a modern Greek Orthodox church.

The Holy Family found refuge in Egypt from the persecution of Herod. The Coptic Church celebrates the memory of the flight of the Holy Family to Egypt on the 24th day of the Coptic month Bashons, corresponding to the first day of June.

The Holy Family crossed the Sinai Peninsula through Rafia, al-Arish and al-Farama. After crossing the narrow isthmus at al-Kantara, the Holy Family passed by Bubastis on Their way to Belbeis in the eastern Delta. Many sources have preserved wonderful details of this flight including the different places blessed by Their presence. Four sites in Cairo claim to be among these places. The best-known site visited by medieval pilgrims and modern tourists is al-Matarya, now a suburb in northern greater Cairo. According to tradition, the Holy Family rested beneath a sycamore tree that is still standing.

The second site is in the district of Babylon where the Holy Family took refuge in a cave. This crypt is beneath the center choir and a part of the central sanctuary of the Church of Abu-Sarga. The crypt chapel has nine columns in two rows, four on the north and five on the south, separating the nave from the two aisles. On the eastern wall is an altar and on the southern a baptistery. This chapel is one of the most ancient Christian monuments in Cairo. The third site in Cairo blessed by the Holy Family can be seen in Haret Zuwaila.

In the floor before the southern sanctuary of the Church of the Virgin is a well. We are told that Christ blessed the water of this well and the Holy Virgin drank from it. The district of Maadi, some kilometers to the south of the Fortress of Babylon, has a church built according to tradition on a site honored by the presence of the Holy Family.

القـاهـرة

العدل رجعوا الى مصر

اذكر يارب من له
نفع بخ ملاكه السمواة

ISLAMIC CAIRO *Dr. Soad Maher*

Cairo has occupied – and still occupies – a prominent position among cities of the world. Since its birth in the Middle Ages, it has never lagged behind the march of civilization. Cairo has evolved as the capital of Egypt and remains so today. Throughout all its successive periods it has been a jewel, and still is, on the forefront of the Orient.

Those who want to write about Cairo should start by studying the history of the three Islamic capitals of Egypt that preceded the establishment of Cairo. It is necessary, not only chronologically and historically, but also because the topography of the new city contained these three capitals.

القَــاهِـرَة

Throughout their conquests, Arabs established new capitals in the conquered lands. The sites for these new Arab towns were chosen to suit the public and private interests of the new rulers.

After the Arab conquest of Egypt, a new capital was built by Amr Ibn el-As in the Year 21 A.H. (After Hejira) – 641 A.D. – north of the Babylon Fortress, where the Muslim troops encamped for the first time. Amr called his new city Al-Fustat. The site of Al-Fustat was well chosen geographically and militarily. It was located at the head of the Nile Delta, where it was protected from enemy attacks. It was also close to Arab lands, which facilitated food provisions. To the east of Al-Fustat was the Muqattam Plateau, its protective shield against enemies. Amr Ibn el-As proved his foresight when he planned his new city so that it could later be extended at its northeastern side.

Having established Al-Fustat, Amr built Al-Atique (the old) mosque in its center. It was the foremost mosque in Africa, "the source of lights; blessed is the man who keeps praying in it and persistently looks after it," wrote Ibn Duqmaq. The mosque was expanded to its present size during the Umayyad period. In the middle of the mosque there is a *sahn* (courtyard) surrounded with arcades on four sides. Its famous minarets are erected above the western arcade (*riwaq*). The stucco decorations of the windows are considered the most beautiful made during the 3rd century of the Hejira.

The mosque was rebuilt in the 7th century A.H. (13th century A.D.). However, the *riwaq* of the prayer niche (the *qibla*) was not rebuilt in its original site; its arches were rebuilt vertically on the *qibla* wall instead of parallel to it as in the original construction.

Within these colonnades the first Islamic university was founded. By the 4th century A.H. there were more than 40 active educational institutions, as well as educational and guidance circles for women. During the Fatimid period, women's circles were led by the esteemed lady, Um el-Khair Al-Hijaziya.

The treasury building (*Bayt el-Mal*) where the orphans' money was kept was located in the middle of the courtyard. In Amr's mosque were also courts where both religious and civil disputes were settled. In the area around the mosque, the Arab tribes designed their living quarters.

Historians and travelers in the Middle Ages gave elaborate descriptions of Al-Fustat. For instance, Al Kudai reported that Fustat had 3,600 mosques, 800 roads and 170 public baths. Though these figures may have been exaggerated, other travelers' books indicated the degree of progress and civilization that had been reached in Al-Fustat, particularly during the Umayyad caliphate when the city was the seat of its rulers.

Unfortunately, only a few ruins remain from the oldest Islamic capital. Al-Fustat was burned in the 6th century A.H. in anticipation of a European occupation. Although the fire burned for 54 days, the remaining relics clearly indicated the civilization and prosperity the city had once enjoyed. Its streets were paved and passable; its houses were well designed and spacious, with five to seven stories each.

The city had sanitary public facilities, including numerous public baths. On a given Friday, the revenue from one bath might have reached 500 dirhams.

Amr has described Egypt as "a dark earth with a green tree within which a blessed river is running with increase or with decrease." Arabs paid a great deal of attention to the Nile. A Nilometer was built in the Island of Roda during the Umayyad period and was rebuilt during the reign of the Abbasid Caliph Al Mutawakkil. It still stands in the southern corner of Roda Island; repaired several times, it is a stone-lined pit that goes well below the level of the Nile. Three tunnels lead into it at different depths. In the center of the pit is a marble column graduated into cubits. When the water rose during flood time, it was possible to tell by the highest point it reached on the column whether the year would be one of too much, too little or just enough water. On wooden panels, Quranic verses are engraved. Running around the pit is a frieze of stone incised with Kufic inscriptions from the 3rd century of Hejira, representing the oldest inscription in the Islamic monuments of Egypt.

Amr's mosque was built by Amr Ibn el-As; hence it was named for him. When Amr made a *minbar* (a pulpit) for his new mosque, he received a message from Caliph Omar Ibn el-Khattab ordering him to remove the *minbar*. Omar wrote: "Is it not enough for you to stand while Muslims are sitting at your feet?" Amr removed the *minbar*, but it was said he brought it back after the death of Omar.

The first addition to the mosque of Amr was carried out in 53 A.H. by Mussallamah Ibn Makhled Al-Ansari, the Wali (the governor) of Egypt during the reign of the Umayyad Caliph Moawiya Ibn Abi Sufiyan. The caliph instructed him to expand the mosque at both its eastern and northern sides. Mussallamah made a courtyard, painted the mosque, and decorated its walls and ceilings.

Moreover, Moawiya ordered that a minaret should be built for the mosque in Fustat, and Mussallamah built four cells, one in each of its four corners. He also was the first one to furnish the mosque with mats instead of gravel.

The second addition took place in the reign of Abdel Aziz Ibn Marwan (79 A.H.), the Umayyad prince of Egypt during the era of the Caliph Abdel Malek Ibn Marwan. Abdel Aziz pulled down the mosque to make room for a new extension toward the west, and the northern yard was included in this addition.

In 175 A.H., during the reign of Haroun el Rasheed, Mousa Ibn Issa added the Abu Ayyoub yard at the back of the mosque. He also widened the road around the mosque.

The mosque reached its present size in 212 A.H. when Abdullah Ibn Taher, prince of Egypt during the rule of the Abbasid Caliph Al Ma'moun, doubled the mosque's area, erected a green panel, restored the roof, built a drinking fountain and constructed the courtyard next to the minting house.

During the Tulunid dynasty most of Ibn Taher's addition as well as the *riwaq* of the green panel were destroyed in a fire. As instructed by Khumarawaih Ibn Ahmad Ibn Tulun, the mosque was restored at the cost of 6,400 dinars. The name of Khumarawaih was recorded in the *riwaq*.

In the Ikhshidid period, most columns were decorated, carved and encircled with silver collars.

In 564 A.H., Al-Fustat was destroyed by fire, and the mosque of Amr was also severely damaged. After Salah el-Din came to power, he ordered the restoration of the mosque. In 568 A.H., the facade was reconstructed, and the large *mihrab* (prayer niche) was covered with marble and his name carved on it.

Throughout the Mameluke period, the mosque was repeatedly renovated. The latest additions were made in 703 A.H. on the western side of the mosque. These are the stucco windows and the exterior stucco *mihrab* with its beautiful inscription band and a highly precise masterpiece of floral decoration. The main restoration was done by Burhan el-Din Ibrahim Ibn Omar Ibn el-Mahalli, the chief of merchants in Egypt at that time. Al-Maqreezi wrote "the Mosque has become new again after it was about to fall down. God sent this man (Burhan), in spite of what was known about his greed, who restored the mosque. May God thank his endeavor and make his face white. Restoration works were completed in 804 A.H. However, no Friday prayer was performed in the mosque during the course of restoration."

The Arab historian Ibn Iyass described the last renovation carried out in the mosque during the Mameluke era: "The Sultan rode down from the Citadel toward the Mosque of Amr Ibn el-As. He inspected the collapsing walls and roofs and gave his instruction to rebuild them at his own expense. The work was immediately started."

As the oldest and the first mosque in Islamic Egypt, the mosque of Amr naturally was a subject of many stories and legends. For instance, people used to tell about certain places inside the mosque in which their prayers are accepted. They also spoke of two adjacent columns on the left of the great northern gate (which is closed now), through which no one could pass unless he was pure. Those who were heavy with sins and faults would try to pass through the two columns in the hope that they might be forgiven. It is usual to see people crowding around these columns after the prayer of the last Friday of Ramadan.

القَاهِرَة

When the Abbasids took over the caliphate, they established a new capital in Egypt. The new city was situated in the northeast of Al-Fustat in a region known as Al-Hamra Al-Kuswa; extending up to the Yashkur hills, it is near the place where Ahmad Ibn Tulun later built his famous mosque. There, the Abbasid army built their houses and lived. Ali Ibn Salih established the governor's headquarters (*Dar al-Emarah*) and soldiers' barracks. Al-Fadl Ibn Salih then built the mosque of Al-Askar in the center of the town.

Eventually, Al-Askar and Al-Fustat became linked to form one

Left: The iwan (prayer place) for the saying of prayers in Amr's mosque, the first to be built in Egypt. Below: The courtyard of the mosque of Ibn Tulun. In its center is a dome mounted on four arches and surrounded by a band of Quranic writing. At the far left is a minaret with three discretely shaped stories: square, circular and octagonal.

large city. Princes of Egypt continued to live in Dar al Emarah in Al-Askar until the establishment of Fatimid Cairo (*Al-Kahira*).

Though there is no evidence of the works that had been carried out or the buildings that had been founded, Al-Maqreezi has elaborately described Al-Askar and its houses, gardens, mosques, markets and public baths. And we do know that Al-Askar was the political capital of Egypt for more than one century (133–256 A.H.).

القَهاِرَة

When Al-Fustat became overpopulated, Ahmad Ibn Tulun founded the new town of Al-Qatai. In its center, he had built a large mosque (*Masjid Jami*) that was completed in the middle of the 3rd century of Hejira. Ibn Tulun's mosque is actually one of the largest in the Islamic world: more than $6\frac{1}{2}$ acres, including its surrounding sanctuary. It is one of the hanging mosques whose doors can be reached by circular staircases. In the center of the mosque is a square courtyard surrounded by two arcades on each of its three sides. The arcades are erected on brick piers with engaged columns. The capitals of the columns are decorated with arabesques.

In the *qibla* wall (which points to Mecca), there are five arcades and five *mihrabs* beside the main central *mihrab*. All *mihrabs* are adorned with beautiful floral, geometrical and calligraphic decorations. The mosque's *mihrabs* date to different ages. One goes back to the Fatimid Caliph al-Mustanser; another *mihrab* belongs to Sultan Lajin. Two other *mihrabs* are situated on the side of the seat of the prayer caller. The one on the right belongs to the Tulunids, while the one on the left dates back to the Fatimids. On the left side of the big *mihrab* is situated a 7th-century *mihrab* belonging to al-Sayyda Nafiesah. Around the upper walls of the mosque is an inscription written in simple Kufic style.

The niche of the main *mihrab* is ornamented with gilded mosaic and Kufic inscriptions.

On the left side of the main *mihrab* is located a wooden *minbar* ornamented with star-like units.

The mosque has 128 stucco window grilles, four of which are original. Arches are crowned with decorated stucco friezes, above which is a wooden band carved with Kufic inscriptions.

In the middle of the courtyard is a large dome mounted on the walls of four arches and surrounded with a band of Quranic

writing. The minaret in the western arcade is the only one in Egypt with a spiral staircase from the outside. The lower story is square, the second circular in plan, the third is octagonal and the upper story is covered with an incense-burner-like *mabkhara*.

Al-Qatai was the first royal city founded in the Nile Valley during the Islamic era. It was the center of an independent ruler whose connection with the Abbasid caliph in Baghdad was purely religious.

The inspiration for Al-Qatai was Samarra in Iraq, where Ibn Tulun had lived before coming to Egypt. Both cities were divided into *qatai* (quarters) in each of which lived a community of people related to each other.

Samarra's style of architecture and decoration seems to have had a great influence on Ibn Tulun – as was quite obvious in the remaining stucco decorations of the Tulunid monuments.

القَهاِرَة

The city of Al-Kahira (Cairo) was founded in 359 A.H. by Gawhar Al-Sikkeli, commander of the Fatimid troops, one year after the Fatimid conquest of Egypt. A wall of clay bricks was built around the city whose sides were each 1,200 yards long. The area enclosed inside the wall was 340 acres. In the center a large palace was constructed on 70 acres. An additional 70 acres were given over to gardens, thoroughfares and squares. The remaining 200 acres were divided into 20 districts and distributed among the army brigades. And a mosque was constructed near the caliph's palace.

The city of Al-Mu'izz li-Din Allah – the first Fatimid caliph in Egypt – was bordered on the east by the Muqattam hills and the gulf of al-Khalig (an irrigating canal that branched off the Nile), now Port-Said Street. Its southern end can be defined by a line drawn from Bab el-Khalq square moving eastward through Bab Zuwila (one of Cairo's old gates).

Cairo began as a modest capital of the Fatimid state and remained for some time a royal city where the caliph's palaces, princes' houses and governmental departments were located.

Since Cairo was the royal city, Egyptians were not allowed to enter it without permission. Cairo's high walls and guarded gates were real barriers between the caliph and his people. During official occasions, commissioners of foreign countries had to get off their horses and walk to the palace between two rows of soldiers.

However, as the emerging city expanded, it soon occupied a remarkable position under the Fatimid caliphs. Its buildings gradually overlapped its walls and reached Al-Fustat. Hence, the two cities became one great city – the largest in the Islamic world during the Middle Ages.

The most important remaining Fatimid monument in Cairo today is the mosque of Al-Azhar, which is considered the first artistic and architectural work built by the Fatimids in Egypt. Al-Azhar lies in the southeast of Al-Mu'izz near the Big Palace, between the Dylam district and the Turkish district to the south.

Al-Azhar has long occupied an esteemed position throughout the Islamic world. It was a lighthouse of science and scholarship until the arrival of the Ayyubids – the orthodox followers of the Sunna. Thus, Friday prayers were abolished in Al-Azhar, but it was continued in el-Hakim mosque in accordance with the Shafei rite. This discrepancy endured for a century until the Mamelukes came to power.

The idea of using Al-Azhar as an educational institution came about as a result of the religious propaganda activities. In time, Al-Azhar evolved into a famous Islamic university. It also had a special official significance as the seat of *Kadhi al-Kudhah* (chief of judges) and the center of *Al-Muhtaseb* (the public auditor), and it was a forum for judicial meetings and debates. Although the Friday prayer was canceled in Al-Azhar during the Ayyubid rule, the mosque continued playing its educational part.

The Mameluke period was the golden age of Al-Azhar, highlighted by its leading position among Islamic scientific centers.

The Ottoman Turkish invasion of Egypt represented the severest blow to Al-Azhar. After the Abbasid caliphate in Baghdad was defeated by the Mongols in the 7th century of Hejira, all intellectual institutions – including Al-Azhar itself – underwent deterioration and even collapse. Nevertheless, the mosque soon became a last resort of theological and religious sciences and a stronghold of Arabic linguistics – a noble task during hard times for Egypt and the entire Islamic world.

As designed by Gawhar Al-Sikelli in 361 A.H. (972 A.D.), Al-Azhar contained only about one-half its present area.

The Fatimid caliphs made many additions to Al-Azhar and many portions have subsequently been renovated over the past few centuries. It is, therefore, difficult to recognize the original plan of the mosque. Nonetheless, there are some bands of Kufic decorations and inscriptions as well as the pointed arches that are characteristic of the Fatimid architecture.

In the northern facade, opposite Al-Azhar square, are the Barbers' Doors, built by Prince Abdul Rahman Katkhuda in 1176 A.H. (1752 A.D.). A passage from the two leads to two schools, the one on the left known as al-Madrassa al-Akbaghawiyah (or eastern); built by Prince Aqbugha Abdel Wahid (740 A.H.–1339 A.D.), it is now occupied by Al-Azhar Library. In this *madrassa* is a *mihrab* whose niche and arch were ornamented with gilded, multicolored mosaic. This *mihrab* is considered one of the most beautiful in Cairo. The second school is al-Madrassa al-Tybarsiyah, built by Tybars al-Ala'i (709 A.H.–1309 A.D.). It is presently an annex of the Library. It also has a beautiful *mihrab* decorated with marble mosaic and very handsome ceramic columns. The facade of this school was restored by Prince Abdul Rahman Katkhuda.

At the end of the passage on the southern side are another door and a minaret, which were established by Sultan Qaitbey in 873 A.H. (1458 A.D.). Stone decoration in both the door and the minaret is highly creative and beautiful (though the door may not be original).

This door leads to an unroofed courtyard surrounded on three sides by arcades. The facades of the arcades are mounted on arches with refracted angles. In the middle of the eastern arcade is a corridor leading vertically to the ancient *mihrab*. Over the entrance of the corridor is a dome mounted on pillars and shoulders. The arches of this corridor are the oldest ones in the arcade. Both the arches and the roof of the corridor are more elevated than the rest of the arcade. The keel arches are decorated with interlaced flowers and floral Kufic inscriptions. In the upper portion of the original wall are old windows distinguished by their circular arches and stucco decorations with geometrical motifs and colored glass. These windows are surrounded by a frieze of Kufic Quranic writings and border the original mosque on three sides. It is believed that the ends of the first arcade were once covered by two domes.

The elevated area behind the recess (or *iwan*) up to the present southern wall was also constructed by Abdul Rahman Katkhuda, whose mausoleum is located west of the palace inside Bab el-Sa'aiyda (Gate of Upper Egyptians).

In 725 A.H. (1324 A.D.) Al-Azhar was renovated by the judge Negm el-Din Mohammad Ibn Hussein Ibn Ali As'udi, the *muhtaseb* of Cairo.

In 740 A.H. the Agbaghawiyah school was built by Prince Ala'a

Left: The three minarets of Al-Azhar mosque. The stone decoration of the central minaret, built by Sultan Qaitbey, is highly creative. The two-crowned minaret on the right, built by Sultan al-Ghouri, is rare in Islamic architecture. Below: The outer gate of Al-Azhar, built by Abdul Rahman Katkhuda, contains distinctive Turkish colored tiles.

el-Din Aqbugha, chief of the Mamelukes under King el-Naser Mohammad Ibn Qalawoon.

In 761 A.H. (1359 A.D.) another restoration was carried out in Al-Azhar when Prince al-Tawashi Saad el-Din Bashir al-Gamdar al-Naseri removed the many chambers that had been introduced to the mosque. He then began to restore all of its walls and roofs. The mosque was painted and the floors were tiled. People were prevented from passing through the mosque. A Quran reader was appointed. At the south gate a *sabil* provided people with fresh drinking water. Above the *sabil*, a *kuttab* (a small Quranic school) was built to teach orphan children the reading of Holy Quran. Daily meals of cooked food were allocated for poor students of Al-Azhar. In addition, teaching circles were arranged at the big *mihrab*.

In 800 A.H. the old minaret of Al-Azhar was pulled down because it was too short to harmonize with the vast mosque. A new, taller minaret was erected by Sultan al-Zahir Barquq. The total expenses were at least 10,000 dirhams of pure silver. When construction was completed that year, a great celebration was held, and the new minaret was completely illuminated with lanterns and candles. Readers and preachers of the mosque held a gathering at which they read the whole Quran and prayed for the sake of the Sultan. This minaret was subsequently removed in 818 A.H. because of architectural defects and a new minaret was made out of stone.

In 884 A.H. (1440 A.D.) Prince Gawhar al-Qanqaba'i, treasurer of King al-Ashraf Bersbay, constructed a beautiful small school at the northern end of the eastern wall of the mosque near Bab el-Sirr. The school, though small, included all the details of the *madrassa*.

The main restoration in Al-Azhar during the period of Sharkasi Mamelukes was done by Sultan Qaitbey in 873 A.H. (1468 A.D.). He pulled down the big old western gate and built the present gate, to the right of which a beautiful new minaret was erected. In 881 A.H. (1476 A.D.) when Sultan Qaitbey visited the mosque, he gave orders to restore the collapsing parts and to remove all the hermitages from the roof.

Despite the cultural deterioration that Al-Azhar suffered during the Ottoman age, Turkish rulers maintained the mosque's physical condition. They also showed great care for Al-Azhar's students and staff. For instance, al-Sharif Mohammad Pasha, a governor in the service of the Ottoman regime, restored the ruined parts of the mosque in 1004 A.H. (1595 A.D.). He also allocated certain amounts of food for the poor, who then came to the mosque from far away.

In 1014 A.H. (1605 A.D.), Hassan Pasha al-Daftardar, another governor, renovated the school of the Hanafites (one of the four Islamic orthodox rites), and covered its floor with tiles.

A great expansion of Al-Azhar took place under the Ottoman Prince Abdul Rahman Katkhuda beginning in 1167 A.H. (1753 A.D.). The area added to the mosque included all the arcades behind the *mihrab*. These arcades now have 50 marble columns supporting 50 stone keel arches. The ceilings are made of wood. This section of the mosque contained a marble *mihrab* covered by a dome. A wooden *minbar* was added, with an octagonal marble panel to its left, carrying rectangular Kufi script of Allah, Mohammad, and the names of the 10 followers to whom paradise was promised. The panel was moved to its present place from the Katkhuda tomb in Al-Azhar. Beside this *mihrab* is a smaller one known as the *mihrab* of al-Dardir. Close by is a third *mihrab*, made by the Department of Preservation of Arabic Monuments to maintain the wooden linings that had covered the old *mihrab*.

Katkhuda also introduced the big gate now known as Bab al-Hallakin (or the Barbers' Door). A minaret was erected to the right of the gate. Above the entrance a *maktab* (or *kuttab*) was built. To the right of the entrance is an ablution fountain with a water wheel.

In 1306 A.H. (1888 A.D.), more restoration work was done on Al-Azhar. The *iwan* built by Katkhuda was renovated and the old eastern *iwan* was largely repaired, as were the al-Saiyda and al-Harmin arcades. Decorations of the arches surrounding the courtyard were restored though their original styles were kept untouched.

In 1890 A.D. portions of the western *iwan* as well as their Kufic inscription bands and stucco decorations were renovated. The Fatimid dome above the entrances was also renovated.

In 1315 A.H. (1898 A.D.) the western facade, including the western Barbers' Gate, was renovated and the Abbassi *ruwaq* was created.

القاهرة

Many Fatimid mosques still exist in present-day Cairo. Among them are al-Aqmar mosque in Al-Mu'izz li-Din Allah at al-Nahhasin, the mosque of Al-Salih Talai near Bab Zuwila, Al-Fakahani mosque at the entrance of Housh Qadam passage at al-

Ghouriya, the sanctuary of el-Guyushi on al-Muqattam hills, the mausoleum of Ekhwat Youssif (Youssif Brothers) at el-Khalifa district and the mausoleum of Sayyda Ruqayia in Khalifa Street.

The city was once surrounded by a wall, which Gawhar had built to protect it from enemy attacks. Though it no longer exists, its position can be approximated by historians' references and archaeologists' findings.

Gawhar opened eight gates in the wall of Cairo, two on each of the four sides. Those on the northern side, which no longer exist, were Bab el-Nasr (The Victory Gate) and Bab el-Futuh (The Conquest Gate).

Bab el-Nasr was located at the crossroads of Bain Al Sayarig and al-Mu'izz streets, 20 meters north of the mosque of el-Shohada (martyrs) known as Wekalat Qussun, in Bab el-Nasr Street near Zawiat al-Kassid.

On the eastern side of the wall were the Bab al-Barqiyah and Bab al-Qarratin gates. According to a map drawn at the time of Napoleon's French Expedition, Bab al-Barqiyah was located at the foot of al-Barqiyah hills opposite to al-Darrassa Street. This gate was named for a group of soldiers who came from Barqah (in Libya) with Gawhar's troops. Bab al-Qarratin was near the present Bab el-Mahrouq at the end of Dar el-Mahrouq in al-Gamaliyah.

Al-Maqreezi reported that al-Bab al-Mahrouq was given its name – the burned gate – because the Mamelukes set fire to it in 652 A.H. after learning that their leader, Prince Aqtai, had been murdered. It was said that they tried to leave the city through this gate one night. But after finding the gate closed, they burned it down and then left.

In the western wall, the two gates of Zuwila referred to a North African Berber tribe whose soldiers joined Gawhar's army while marching toward Egypt. The site of the two gates was said to be at the mosque of Ibn el-Banna.

On the site of these two gates now stands Bab Zuwila, a large gate built by Badr al-Gemali. People call it al-Metwali Gate, "Bawabet al-Metwali," because the Metwali – the man who was responsible for collecting taxes from those coming to Cairo – used to sit there.

On the western side of the walls, parallel to Khalig Amir el-Mu'menin were the two gates of Sa'ada and al-Qantara. Sa'ada gate was related to Sa'ada Ibn Hayyan, one of al-Mu'izz's officers. The gate was 10 meters to the north of the Court of Appeals (now the headquarters of the Ministry of Municipalities). Bab al-Qantara was located at the entrance of Amir el-Gu'yoush el-Guwani Street. It was so called because Gawhar built an arched bridge on the Khalig (or the gulf) on which the army could pass on its way to al-Maqs, a Nile harbor, to fight against al-Qramitah's incursions.

Added to the wall around Cairo and the mosque of Al-Azhar in its center, Gawhar built a great palace near Al-Azhar. It was said that the foundations of the Great Eastern Palace were laid on the same night as those of the wall. Work continued for four years until the palace was ready to receive the Caliph al-Mu'izz.

The palace reportedly had 4,000 rooms well furnished and rich in ornaments, jewels, draperies, receptacles and arms. The palace was virtually a complex of palaces brought together in one huge building. However, when al-Aziz came to power, he built the smaller Western Palace. Between the two palaces a vast yard was left; it was said that 10,000 soldiers were able to stand in it. Interior courtyards, roof gardens, galleries and other annexes of the two palaces covered 70 acres.

Medieval historians and travelers have given rich descriptions of the architecture of these palaces and their luxurious furnishings.

Unfortunately, these palaces were soon destroyed due to the political instability that prevailed because of the hostility between the Sunnite Ayyubids and Shia Fatimids. The Great Palace gave way to the el-Salihya and el-Zahiryah schools, the *sabil* of Mohammad Ali (al-Nahhasin School), Beshkat Palace, al-Gamaliya police station and its environs, most of which are now in al-Mu'izz Street. The Western Palace was replaced by the mosques of el-Mansour Qalawoon and his son el-Naser, the mosque of al-Zahir Barqouq and al-Kamaliyah School. Inside these Mameluke buildings, which still exist, is a good deal of woodwork that had been taken from Fatimid palaces. The woodwork contains relief carvings representing dancing and singing parties, hunting scenes, birds and animals. They tell us something about the social life in the Fatimid period.

When Naser Khisro, the traveler, arrived in Egypt during the reign of the Caliph al-Mustanser in 439 A.H., he noted that the wall built by Gawhar in 358 A.H. had crumbled, only 80 years after it had been established. Since Cairo had no walls at the beginning of al-Mustanser's rule, his vizier (or prime minister) Badr el-Gemali undertook the fortification of Cairo against foreign invasions and rioting soldiers. A new wall was built instead of the ruined wall of Gawhar.

Left: The entrance of El-Moaed mosque with its famous door taken from the madrassa of Sultan Hassan. Below: Bab el-Futuh (the Conquest Gate), located in the north wall of Old Cairo. The arched portal of the gate contains a hole from which liquids could be poured over an attacking enemy.

The site of el-Gemali's wall can still be identified from its remnants, the most important of which are the three gates: Bab el-Nasr and Bab el-Futuh to the north, and Bab Zuwila to the south. These gates are among the finest examples of medieval military fortifications.

Bab el-Futuh contains two cylindrical towers; the lower two-thirds of each is solid while the upper third had soldiers' chambers and slits from which arrows could be shot. Between the two towers is an arched portal with a hole above from which liquids could be poured over the attacking enemy.

Bab el-Nasr has two square towers whose stones are decorated with reliefs representing shields, armor and other weapons. In the middle, it has an elevated gate with an opening from which burning liquids could be poured. Both towers are solid in the lower two-thirds, and are encircled by a flowered Kufic band listing the founder's name and the date of construction.

Bab el-Nasr is connected to Bab el-Futuh by two vaulted galleries with domed chambers and arrow slits on its sides.

The most beautiful of the three gates is Bab Zuwila. It has two cylindrical towers similar to those of Bab el-Futuh. Yet, the upper third of each tower was removed in 818 A.H. by King al'Mu'ayad Abul Nasr Sheikh when he built his mosque beside the gate and built two minarets on the towers.

During the Fatimid period, social life in Cairo was said to be prosperous, lively and cheerful. The Fatimid luxury was beyond imagining. After 200 years, at the end of the Fatimid monarchy, Cairo became a large city full of houses, markets, entertainment, mosques, palaces, mausolea and parks. Surviving buildings and monuments are a good witness of that era.

القاهرة

Egypt remained under the Ayyubids for only about 80 years, during which the city was rich with beautiful buildings and the most refined Islamic arts. Although most of these monuments no longer exist, the ones that remain provide evidence of the progress and prosperity of the arts at that time and their architectural influences on the buildings established in later eras. During that period the multi-rite religious schools (or *madrassa*), with their characteristic square architectural details, appeared in Egypt. Meanwhile, many military fortifications such as citadels and fortified walls as well as public works, like the barrages of Giza, were also established by the Ayyubid sultans.

During this brief time in Cairo, Salah el-Din left several monuments that demonstrate his wisdom, political insight and military skill.

The most important of them is the Citadel – or the Mountain Citadel as it has been commonly known – built on a big rock split off the Muqattam hills, to the east of Cairo. The Citadel overlooked the capital of Salah el-Din's empire, protecting it from any expected invasion, and providing a headquarters for the sultan. The Citadel was built on the same spot where the Abbasids had once established el-Hawa dome (the dome of the air) in the 2nd century of Hejira. Salah el-Din ordered a residential palace to be built for him, and Yosif's well provided the Citadel with water in times of war or siege.

His vizier Baha'a el-Din Qaraqoush was given the responsibility for building both the Citadel and the wall. Though Salah el-Din died before completing his plans, they came to fruition during the rule of his brother, Sultan al-Adel.

Since that time, the Citadel has been the royal headquarters of all the successive rulers of Egypt until Khedive Ismail moved to Abdin Palace in 1850 A.D. Over the centuries, the Citadel has undergone additions.

The continuous wars in which Salah el-Din was involved had their obvious influence on the construction carried out during his lifetime. Having established the Citadel, he started to encircle all the previous Islamic capitals of Egypt as well as his Citadel with a single wall extending from Fatimid Cairo in the north up to the south of Al-Fustat. Many parts of this wall still exist today.

The present-day Citadel is practically a great town surrounded by huge walls and towers on all sides. The Citadel can be divided into two distinguishing parts, the northeastern and the southwestern. Each part has walls on all four sides. The two parts are connected by a joint wall.

The features of the southwestern section clearly indicate that it underwent many changes and much reconstruction from the time of Salah el-Din to that of Mohammad Ali. On the other hand, there is a great harmony in the walls of the northeastern section, and archaeologists have proved that this section was constructed during the Ayyubid dynasty itself.

The northeastern section is confined in a trapezoidal shape. Its length from east to west reaches 560 meters, and its width from north to south is 317 meters. The circumference is approximately 2,000 meters. The joint wall – between north and south – extends to 150 meters. It is huge, a thick wall culminating in two great towers with the Bab el-Kullah in the middle.

The southwestern section, which is slightly smaller than the first one, is irregular in shape, and is separated from the northern part by an acute angle. Its maximum length from north to south is 510 meters, and the maximum width from east to west is 240 meters. While the northern walls are supported by several circular and semi-circular towers, the southern walls are uninterrupted by any towers.

The interiors of the two sections are also different. While the northern section has the rough features of a military fortress, the southern section resembles a royal city with its mosques and palaces.

During the ages following the Ayyubids, expansions were made in the fortifications and in the civilian buildings, including houses and palaces.

During the Ottoman rule, the Citadel continued to be the headquarters of Egypt's rulers, and the Ottoman governors added many buildings.

When Mohammad Ali came to power, he restored the Citadel to its former glory. He founded several buildings inside the Citadel, the most important of which are the mosque of Mohammad Ali (1262 A.H.–1845 A.D.), the Mint, the Archives House (Dar al-Mahfouzat), the Gawhara Palace, the Palace of Justice (1262 A.H.–1811 A.D.) and the palaces of the Harem (among which is the palace presently occupied by the Military Museum).

The Citadel continued to be the focus of the rulers' attention as the center of power and authority. But after Khedive Ismail moved to his new headquarters, the Citadel began to deteriorate. This decline has recently intensified, due in part to environmental pollution and other modern encroachments.

Thanks to Salah el-Din, the religious schools – in which the four Islamic Sunnite rites were taught – were modeled after the schools built by Nour el-Din Zinki in Syria. The main point of these schools was to counter the Shiite thought that prevailed under the Fatimids. The architecture of the madrassa was completely different from that of the mosque. The madrassa consists of four iwans surrounding a small courtyard, often with a fountain in its center. In each iwan one of the four rites of Islam was taught. Parts of the madrassa were often used as residences by either the teachers or students. There were also libraries and lecture halls.

Among the religious buildings from the Ayyubid period is the dome of Imam al-Shafei, which includes significant architectural details, especially in the style of the interior decorations of the dome. The dome is distinguished by its muqarnas (squinches) with their characteristic floral and geometric decorative style.

القَاهِرَة

Egypt was ruled by sultans of Bahrite Mamelukes for about 100 years. In spite of the violent and arbitrary character of the Mameluke rule, their era was a prosperous one in the architectural history of Cairo. Their love of fine arts was obvious in their civil and religious buildings alike, as in their furniture and dress. Museums and private collections all over the world have examples of outstanding Egyptian monuments and masterpieces that clearly show the extent of the richness, prosperity and refinement that Cairo reached under their rule.

Cairo itself has many buildings that date from this era, including an outstanding collection of great mosques with their skyscraping minarets. Just as Pharaonic Egypt had the pyramids, Islamic Egypt can be proud of Sultan Hassan's madrassa, an incomparable building among all the countries of Islam.

Though the buildings of the Bahrite Mamelukes differ in their geometrical details and architectural decorations, they do have some common characteristics.

While mosques and other religious structures from former ages are characterized by their simplicity and lack of external decorations, the facades of Mameluke buildings are rich in friezes, cornices, crowns and other elements of architectural decorations. Minarets of Mameluke mosques are more elegant and finer than earlier ones. They are made out of carved stones, and their bases are octagonal, and later cylindrical, rather than squares. The waists of the minarets have been ornamented with fringes that make them more beautiful and charming. It might be said that the Mamelukes were dome builders. During their era, the horizons of Cairo were full of domes and cupolas erected over mihrabs and entrances of the mosques. The simple dome developed a more complicated shape, with a lobed cupola above the dome, or a dome made from carved stone, and decorated with accurately interlaced geometrical and structural forms.

Buildings of the era of Sultan el-Naser are distinguished by the stone facades in two colors, a style called al-ablaq (piebald). On

Bab el-Nasr (left) and Bab el-Futuh, two fine examples of medieval military fortifications. The gates are remnants of a wall built to fortify Cairo against invasions.

*Below: The mosque of Gawhar El-Lallah, a minister of
Sultan Hassan who himself became sultan after Hassan's exile.
Right: The dome of ablution in the center of the courtyard of the
madrassa of Sultan Hassan. The courtyard is surrounded by the
four iwans where the Islamic Orthodox rites are conducted.*

*Overleaf: An exterior view of the madrassa of Sultan Hassan with
its dome and minaret built during the 7th century A.H.*

Left: The mihrab *of the* madrassa *of Sultan Hassan with its rare gilded inscriptions. Below: The* mihrab *of el-Hakim, one of the important Fatimid mosques, built in 401 A.H.*

Below: The complex of Sultan Barqouq, which includes his mosque and khanqah, *a building used for religious instruction. Right: the mosque of Ibn Qalawoon with its beautiful astral designs and bands of calligraphy.*

certain occasions, black-and-white marble was used. Facades were decorated from the outside with ornamented Arabic calligraphy in comparison with earlier periods when decoration was only internal. Ceilings were now made of wood with the supporting beams gilded or oil-painted in a wonderfully harmonious and balanced frame. Buildings began to be illuminated at night by lanterns made of copper or bronze inlaid with silver and gold, or by enameled glass lamps (*mishkah*).

Construction during Mameluke times also included aqueducts, barrages and water wells. Among the most important of these works is the aqueduct established by el-Naser Mohammad Ibn Qalawoon to provide the Citadel with Nile water. This aqueduct, known as *Magra al-Iuoun*, is one of the most outstanding medieval monuments still existing in Cairo.

At the instructions of el-Naser Mohammad Ibn Qalawoon, a well was dug along the Nile and a new barrage was connected up to an existing aqueduct by the ancient barrages in Salah el-Din Wall. In that manner, water collected from the two wells supplied the Citadel. The aqueduct was restored twice: once by Prince Yalbugha al-Salemi in 812 A.H., and again in 911 A.H. by Sultan al-Ghouri. During the Ottoman era, the aqueduct was partially repaired by Abdi Pasha in 1140 A.H. Napoleon's troops later blocked most of the arches in the aqueduct and used it as a defensive wall. The present aqueduct, which extends from Fumm el-Khalig to Bab el-Sayyda Aisha, is about 3.1 km. long, and the cornice now separates the Nile from the head of the aqueduct. The aqueduct then runs eastward to Sabil al-Wassiyah near Qaitbey Gate, before turning to the northeast, past al-Zumor mosque, to the gate of al-Sayyda Aisha.

The aqueduct is mounted on bridges; of the 271 remaining arches, most are circular. The aqueduct has undergone several restorations as a result of deterioration and after being used as a military fortification during the French Expedition.

The head of the aqueduct is an unequal hexagon with an area of 625 square meters. Inside it is an equal-sided hexagon with a column in its center and six raised arches surrounding it. These arches are slightly wider than the hexagon and are uncovered. A sloping ramp leads to the roof where animals were brought to run the water wheels. The roof contains a basin in which water was gathered, before being poured into a ditch, and running from it to the rest of the barrages.

The *madrassa* of Sarghatmish, named for the chief of the Mamelukes during the reign of King al-Muzaffar Haji Ibn Mohammad Ibn Qalawoon, was founded in the year 757 A.H. as a teaching center for the Hanafi rite. Located adjacent to the western sanctuary of Ibn Tulun's mosque, the *madrassa* is noteworthy for its Persian-style architecture. It consists of an unroofed *sahn* surrounded by four *iwans*. In the center of the courtyard is a fountain surrounded by eight marble columns. In the eastern *iwan* are four doors, two of which lead to hermitages and the other two to the teaching halls. The *madrassa* is the only one in existence with a dome above the *mihrab*. It also has wooden stalactites. The minaret is built of stone, 40 meters high, with three levels. The lower two are octagonal while the third level consists of marble columns with beautiful and elegant *muqarnas* topped by a carved crown. On the second level, the white stones are inlaid with red stones in a beautiful decorative piebald pattern. The minaret has a balcony on one side of its lower base, unlike other minarets of the time that had four balconies.

The Mameluke age was responsible for one of Islam's architectural wonders, the mosque and *madrassa* of Sultan Hassan. The huge complex gathers into a whole structural excellence, artistry, the precision of its geometry, and the harmony of decorations in stone, marble, wood, copper, gold, silver, and stained and enameled glass.

The *madrassa* is located at the foot of the Citadel on a site formerly occupied by one of the most beautiful Mameluke palaces. This palace, founded by King el-Naser Mohammad Ibn Qalawoon for Prince Yulbugha al-Behyadi, was razed, and the new complex began construction in the year 757 A.H. Over the next 10 years, Sultan Hassan allocated tremendous amounts of money on the *madrassa*, nearly exhausting the treasury and leaving him in doubt over whether the work should continue.

The plan of the *madrassa* is cruciform, having four main sections with a central uncovered courtyard in the middle of which is an ablution fountain covered by a wooden dome. The original design allowed for four minarets but only two were finally erected. The *madrassa* is actually a polygon with an area of about two acres including the dome adjacent to the eastern facade. Around the courtyard, there are four schools for the four Islamic rites. Each school consists of an *iwan* (or teaching hall), a courtyard with a central fountain and a number of stories looking over the small courtyard from one side and over the facade of the great *madrassa* from the other side.

The discipline of study in these schools was similar to that followed in the 20th-century schools. For each school, a sheikh (or a headmaster) was appointed by the sultan; in addition, there were teachers of the Quran and the Hadith (the sayings of the Prophet), a reader of the Quran, and two tutors. Each school had a library and a librarian. One hundred students were admitted to the boarding school, including 25 advanced students. Thirty students acted as heads of students and others prayed for the sultan at the end of each day's lessons. Two *kuttabs* (small schools for teaching) were annexed to the *madrassa* to enable orphans to learn the Quran and Arabic calligraphy. The children were provided with food and clothing. When an orphan memorized the Quran, he and his teacher each received 50 dirhams. A physician, an opthalmologist and a surgeon were appointed to provide students with medical care. Sultan Hassan allocated suitable *wakfs* (or trusts) for the school's expenses, including the salaries of students, teachers and employees.

The *madrassa* of Sultan Hassan was used as a military fortress in times of political instability, strife and turmoil. In the year 791 A.H. cannons were installed on its roof, and from there the Citadel was shelled in the course of fighting between two conflicting Mameluke groups. The fighting was so frequent that Sultan Barqouq ordered the removal of the stairs leading to the roof. Combatants subsequently used minaret staircases to reach the roof. The *madrassa* of Sultan Hassan became a target of the Citadel's cannons, leading to much devastation and plunder.

القَـاهِـرَة

Among the important religious buildings in Egypt during the Mameluke time were the *khanqahs* (or monasteries), which gained fame throughout the Islamic world, particularly in Iran, in the 4th century of Hejira. The *khanqah* is a house for the accommodation of Sufis or al-*Mutsawifa* (the devotees) who dedicated themselves to worship.

Concerning the emergence of Sufism, or Islamic mysticism, al-Qushairi stated that "following the death of the Prophet Mohammad, Muslims showed great respect to the Prophet's companions who were known as *al-sahaba*; the second generation of Muslims who followed the *sahaba* were known as *al-tabi'een*, or the followers. Those who expressed a great deal of attention towards the religion were called the devotees, because they voluntarily renounced the worldly pleasures and devoted their life to the service of Islam. They have become famous as *Sufis*."

According to another opinion, Sufism evolved in Islam among those who spent their days in worship and prayer in the Prophet's mosque. A third point of view refers the term Sufi to *al-Safaa*, which means clearness – specifically spiritual clearness.

Al-Gahez first used the term *Sufi* to describe many of the devotees who were famous for the purity of their Arabic. Later in the 2nd century of Hejira, the terms *Sufi* and *Mutasawif* became commonly used. This period marked a transition in the development of Sufism. At this time, Sufis only differed from other Muslims in their more pronounced devotion to certain Quranic rules. The most outstanding Sufi of this period was al-Hassan al-Basri, who used to hold study circles in the Friday mosque of al-Basra, at which he discussed various theological viewpoints and encouraged spiritual education.

During this second century, some hard-line Sufis began to show an extreme interest in spiritual exercises and renounced the pleasures of life as a trivial struggle for evanescent things.

By the 3rd and 4th centuries of Hejira, Sufism was no longer restricted to abstinence and devoutness, but had developed its intellectual and spiritual principles. A long-standing ideological dispute erupted between Sufis and many other religious thinkers. This conflict was not limited to books and theses, but escalated into repression against the Sufis. Their recourse was to create a symbolic language understood only by their partisans and scholars.

They also began to organize themselves into groups similar to political parties. Each group had its own principles, fundamentals, leader and followers. Each Sufi had to obey his sheikh.

As their numbers increased, they became a significant faction in Islamic society, with their own traditions, regulations and qualities. They then formed *khanqahs* or *khawanek* where they could gather.

The early fundamentals for regulating the *khanqahs* were laid down by Abu Saed Ibn Abi el-Khair, who became known as the "Father of Khanqahs" and "The Hawk of the Way."

By the 5th century of Hejira, there was a considerable body of Sufi literature, and its traditions and regulations provided models for education and public manners. Respect for Sufis was shown by rulers such as Sultan Mahmoud al-Ghaznawi, who used to pay visits to Sheikh Abdul Hassan al-Kharqanah in his own *khanqah* at al-Rayy.

The 6th century of Hejira was the springtime of prosperous Sufism. *Khanqahs* proliferated throughout the Islamic world.

Sufism was practiced by people in all classes of society. Its principles and foundations became well-known and became the subjects of poems and songs. Kings and sultans – such as Al-Khiushani and Salah el-Din – invited Sufi leaders to their intimate meetings and listened to their advice. Having gained widespread respect, the Sufis even tried to mediate between the different Muslim sects, especially between Sunna and Shia.

The *khanqah* of Saed el-Soada is considered the first to have been founded in Egypt. It was established in the 6th century of Hejira by Salah el-Din for poor Sufis from abroad, and it was known as "the little house of Sufis."

After the Mongols flooded Persia and Iraq during the 7th century of Hejira, Sufi immigrants fled to the western parts of the Islamic world in large numbers, and many settled in Egypt. At one time, Egypt had 21 *khanqahs*, and today eight from that period still exist: al-Bunduqdariyah, al-Gawliyah, al-Baybarsiyah, al-Shrabishiyah, al-Gibgha, al-Muzaffari, Khanqah Syriaqous and Khanqah of Arslan.

The Mameluke *khanqahs* in Egypt date from the 8th century. In addition to their original functions they were used for religious courses. For example, the rite of Imam al-Shafi was taught in the *khanqah* of al-Gawliyah; the al-Hanafi rite was learned in al-Gamaliyah Khanqah; and the four Islamic rites, the reading of the Quran and interpretations of the Prophet Hadith were all taught in Shikhuniah.

Other *khanqahs* remained loyal to their fundamentalist traditions such as the performance of Friday prayer in certain Friday mosques. For example, the Sufis of Beybars *khanqah* used to pray in the mosque of el-Hakim adjacent to their *khanqah*.

القَاهِرَة

The Egyptian Department of Antiquities has shown great interest in the restoration of houses and palaces from the time of the Bahrite Mamelukes.

Al-Ablaq Palace was founded by Sultan el-Naser Mohammad Ibn Qalawoon inside the Citadel of Salah el-Din, in the southern part of the Banner Yard. The palace contains a *durka'a* (a rectangular low-floored hall) with an octagonal fountain in the center. On two sides of the hall, the floor is raised. A door on the north corner leads to a spiral staircase and to an underground passage. The western door leads to a staircase and an uncovered passage; both of them may connect up with the tunnel leading to the relics of the palaces located beneath the mosque of Mohammad Ali. West of the hall is the main *iwan* of al-Ablaq Palace with its floor 30 cm. higher than that of the hall.

Beshtak Palace was founded by Prince Seif el-Din Beshtak al-Naseri, a prince in the time of King el-Naser Mohammad Ibn Qalawoon. It was located in the vicinity of the Fatimid Eastern Big Palace and was accessible through Bab el-Bahr (The Gate of the Sea), later known as the Gate of Beshtak Palace. Historians considered the palace one of the greatest in Cairo. It had windows with iron grilles that looked out over Cairo. The marble work was wonderful. On the ground floor were stores for selling sweets and other things.

The construction of the palace was completed in the year 738 A.H. Despite its grandeur, Beshtak hated the palace, and so he sold it to the wife of Prince Buktomor al-Saqi. The palace's ownership moved among their heirs until Sultan el-Naser Hassan, son of Mohammad Ibn Qalawoon, came to power. The palace settled under the ownership of his sons. At last, Ustadar Gamal el-Din had it razed, but his family retained the property.

القَاهِرَة

At the time Sultan Barqouq came to power, rulers of Egypt were known as Circassian Mamelukes; they took their name from the homeland of Barqouq. Although Egypt was suffering from internal instability and the oppressive character of the Circassian Mamelukes, under their rule it reached unprecedented heights in the arts and civilization. This reflected the Mamelukes' interest in the arts, literature, science and religion. Their good taste was manifested in their style of life and their architecture. For instance, kings Barqouq, al-Muayyad and Qaitbey were all fond of taking part in the forums of thinkers and writers. King al-Zahir Tamarbugha was known for his wide knowledge of the origins of languages, history and Sufism. The kings also abided by the religious rules, which included abstaining from alcoholic beverages and making the pilgrimage to Mecca.

Cairo has retained many of its structures from that time, and they provide good examples of the development of religious and civil architecture. They also demonstrate the high level of applied arts and design during the 9th and 10th centuries of the Hejira in Egypt.

A distinctive new art was born in this period when engraved decorated stone replaced decorated plaster. The stone *minbar* of Qaitbey in the mausoleum of Barqouq is one of the outstanding examples of stone carving in the 15th century A.D. It is so intricate that it resembles a piece of lacework.

Circassians differ from Bahrites in both their origins and their system of succession. All Circassian sultans were Turks with the exception of two Greeks. Moreover, Circassians had no firmly established principle of hereditary succession like that of the Qalawoons. The sultan was considered as the chief of Mamelukes, or their leader rather than a "king." The Mamelukes, in fact, elected the sultan. The authority of the sultan totally depended on the strength of his army and his military skills. At the same time, his political experience, proficiency, self-dependence and ability to control the conflicting Mameluke groups all had great influence on his success or failure.

When the sultan died, his followers formed their own party, giving it the title of the late sultan. Hence the names: Ashrafiya, Naseriyah, Muaiadyah and Tahiriyah.

Of the 29 Circassian sultans, six ruled for a total of 103 out of the 134 years the Circassians were in power. Since the era was one of frequent and bloody struggles for power, a Mameluke leader had to be efficient and strong to reach the throne of Egypt. Once a Mameluke became a sultan, he had to leave his position in the army; the one exception was Sultan Farag, a famous general.

Circassian sultans left several monuments, including mosques, hospitals, schools and colleges. Nonetheless, Egypt suffered from the conflicts between Mameluke groups and their bloody competitions for the seat of sultan. As foreign rulers, the Mamelukes were indifferent to the Egyptian people.

The injustice and corruption of Mameluke soldiers were also so flagrant that women were not able to go out of their houses to shop, or to attend weddings or even funerals. Farmers lived in terror, unable to enter the markets of Cairo to buy their crops or their cattle for fear of being plundered by the Mamelukes or – at the very least – selling their goods at low prices to meet the huge requirements of the sultan's palaces. It was said that, for instance, 1,200 pounds of beef were consumed daily in the palace of Bersbay.

Government administration was corrupt, unjust and in-effectual. Judges were dishonest and unfair. On rare occasions, people were able to revenge themselves on their despotic governors. But in most cases they underwent terrible suffering.

Accordingly, social unrest and instability were frequent, especially during tax-collection season or when the country was preparing for war. These calamities were aggravated by plagues or by natural catastrophes such as floods and droughts. Under the reign of Sultan Farag, the population of Egypt was reportedly reduced by two-thirds. Another Circassian sultan, Muaiad Sheikh, was a good and modest man, a lover of music and poetry, builder of a mosque, a hospital and many schools; even so, he failed to protect the people from his followers' excesses.

Under Khushkadam, a Circassian king of Greek ancestry, corruption was at its worst. The government added to its revenues by selling official jobs. The governor of Tripoli paid 45,000 dinars to receive a better post as a governor of Damascus. Another prince paid 10,000 dinars to replace him in Tripoli. On another occasion, the sultan invited a rich prince for a royal banquet; before the night had ended, the guest was forced to pay a sum of money to his host as ransom.

Nevertheless, the Mamelukes did succeed in keeping Egypt free from foreign invaders, particularly against the Mongols who devastated Iraq and parts of Syria. Thanks to Sultan Barqouq and his son, Sultan Farag, their strong army stopped the march of Tamerlane toward Egypt in the year 1400 A.D.

During this period, however, a succession of civil wars and bloody struggles for power caused the decline of political authority and deterioration of the economy. This condition prevailed until the emergence of a strong prince, Sultan Qaitbey, who returned Egypt to stability.

The 29-year reign of Sultan Qaitbey was one of the longest of the Circassian Mameluke era. He stood out as the Circassians' most powerful and courageous ruler, and his political experience and military skills enabled him to impose discipline and order until the final years of his rule. By that time the state economy had been depleted by continual wars and the need for military fortifications, as well as a plague, which brought mass death to Egypt. While conflicts between the Mamelukes escalated once more, King Qaitbey died, a saddened man in his 80s. After four kings ruled for only five years of constant turmoil, a strong, experienced, 60-year old ruler, Al Ashraf Qansuwah al-Ghouri, came to power. His first tasks as ruler were to bring security and order to Cairo, and to refill the state coffers, though poverty was still widespread.

Al-Ghouri put a great deal of money into new buildings and public facilities; he established a *madrassa*, a dome and other

Left: A balcony with arabesque design from the house of Hussein el-Sehemi, a merchant during the Ottoman period in the 18th century A.D. Below: The garden of el-Sehemi house.

buildings in the area known now as Al-Ghouriyah. He reconstructed the road of pilgrimage to Mecca, built way-stations and cleaned the wells along the road. He fortified Alexandria and Rasheed with citadels and towers and restored Salah el-Din's Citadel. At that time, the royal court was very rich and luxurious.

The most remarkable feature of the religious structures from this period is their modest size – especially those built inside the walls of the old city of Cairo. Of course, a small *madrassa* or *khanqah* could only accommodate small *iwans*. Accordingly, the north and south *iwans* of contemporary mosques became known as the two niches. In addition, study in schools of the Circassian age was limited to two rites only, and so the new *madrassas* came to have two large *iwans*, the *iwan* of the *qibla* and another one opposite it, as well as two other small *iwans*.

Similarly, the area of the courtyard was reduced, and the new *sahn* was covered by a wooden roof that usually had a central octagonal skylight (or *shukhshekha*). The new wooden floor gave a special significance to the courtyard. Architects surrounded the roof with Mameluke-style inscription bands, usually beginning with Quranic verses and ending with memorial texts recording the name of the founder, his title and the date of its foundation. Since the floor of the courtyard is usually 25 cm. lower than those of the *iwans*, the new *sahn* acquired the term *durka'a*.

Since the northern and southern *iwans* were reduced in size, the *qibla iwan* became greater than it had been before, occupying its whole wall.

There was no longer a need for four doors in the courtyard, and doors could lead from one room to another. Niches became more frequent, especially in the western *iwan* opposite the *qibla's*. The western *iwan* had a large niche occupied by the platform (or *dekka*) of the messenger. The *dekka* was now usually made of marble or stone rather than wood, and was supported by piers of marble, usually in the shape of a palm-leaf fan; it was reached by an external staircase behind the *iwan*. The arches of the *iwans* were decorated with fine floral forms carved in stone, similar to those found in the metallic monuments and famous inlaid doors dating from the Mameluke age.

The late Mameluke period was distinguished by a new type of dome that was used as a resting place and for entertainment and sports. It was very similar to the domes built by the Fatimids in the suburbs of Cairo and in the rural areas; the best examples are the domes of Yashak Ibn Mahdi in Kubri al-Kobba, and al-Kubba al-Fedewiyyah in Abbassia Square.

The Circassian Mamelukes achieved architectural fame for the multi-crowned minarets, which were unique in Egypt. This type of minaret appeared for the first time in Egypt in the second half of the 8th century of Hejira, and became common in the 9th and early 10th centuries.

One of the earliest examples was the mosque of Junbulat adjacent to Bab el-Nasr, north of Fatimid Cairo. The minaret of Kany Bey al-Rammah's school near the citadel, which was built in 908 A.H., also had two crowns. This minaret was reconstructed according to its original design in the year 1278 A.H./1870 A.D. The same architect had another double-crowned minaret in his *madrassa* in al-Naseriyah, which is still in its original state.

The minaret of al-Ghouri's *madrassa* was the first one in Egypt with four crowns. It was cited in the document of its *wakf* that "in its western corner there is a minaret of three stories. The upper story has four semi-domes, each of which is independent, supported by four piers, and has three columns in the shape of a candlestick."

It is noteworthy that the Committee for the Preservation of Islamic Monuments has renovated the minaret of al-Ghouri and rebuilt its upper part with four crowns instead of two.

Al-Ghouri constructed another minaret in Al-Azhar mosque in the year 915 A.H. characterized by its double crown. It resembles the minaret of Azbak al-Yosofi, near Ibn Tulun, built in 900 A.H., as well as the minaret of Khayer Bek's mosque.

The only multi-crowned minaret from the Ottoman period is that of Mohammad Abdul Dahab's mosque in Al-Azhar square, which was built in the year 1188 A.H./1774 A.D.

القاهرة

After the Mamelukes were defeated, Sultan Selim took over Egypt in the year 923 A.H. (1517 A.D.). Cairo then changed from the capital of a vast empire to the capital of a dependency ruled by Istanbul, and it remained under Ottoman rule until World War I three centuries later.

Having conquered the Mamelukes, Selim stayed in Cairo for eight months while he established a regime to keep Egypt under his firm control. Selim divided the power among three competitive authorities: Al-Wali, the governor who ruled Egypt in the name of the Ottoman sultan; Al-Diwan, an assembly formed of high officers of the Turkish occupation troops; and the

Mamelukes, the former rulers of Egypt. Al-Wali had the title of pasha, and was ensconced in the citadel. He was mainly responsible for implementing the sultan's orders.

Governors were assigned to Cairo for no more than three years, and they often dedicated themselves to accumulating as much wealth as they could during this short period of time. Since the money that was collected as taxes was supposed to be sent to Istanbul, there were frequent disputes between the Wali and Diwan or between the Wali and the king himself over money problems.

The Diwan consisted of leaders of the occupation army, who held their meetings in the Citadel. Their main task was to keep an eye on Al-Wali, while providing him with necessary assistance. The occupation troops had great influence in the early period of the Ottoman rule. The army frequently disobeyed the Wali and more than once drove him out of office – or even killed him. So, many Walis were mere puppets in the hands of the army commanders.

When Sultan Selim took over Egypt, he appointed a few of the surviving Mamelukes as provincial governors, and others were given high positions in the Government. Although there were at most 10,000 Mamelukes in Cairo at that time, they constituted an aristocracy, living in magnificent palaces and enjoying great luxury. They bought children to be slaves. The boys were trained to ride horses, fight, hunt and learn the principles of Islam. When a male slave grew up, his master would emancipate him, and he could adopt the title of Bek in a magnificent celebration. He then became a follower of his master.

The Mamelukes' influence increased as a result of the weakness of the Ottoman state after the end of the 17th century, the continually changing Walis, and the frequent conflicts between the Wali and the Diwan. Under such conditions, the chief of the Mamelukes – Sheikh el-Balad – became the real ruler of Egypt with power to dismiss the Wali if he saw fit.

Having set up a ruling regime for Egypt, Selim I transported from Cairo to Istanbul weapons, books, rare manuscripts and other precious things. He also sent 1800 skilled artisans to Istanbul, depriving Egypt of their workmanship. Therefore, the arts in Cairo suffered.

Selim also removed the last Abbasid caliph to Istanbul, forcing him to renounce his office and transferring the caliphate to the Ottomans.

In the early Ottoman period, while the country enjoyed economic prosperity, Cairo was full of bazaars, *wekalat*, inns, hotels and public baths. Although the Portuguese discovered the sea route via the Cape of Good Hope to India in the 16th century A.D., a great part of the transit trade to India and the Orient still passed through Egypt, and goods from Venice, Genoa and Marseilles continued to flow into Cairo's markets. And the merchants of Cairo constituted a strongly organized community.

Yet, in the year 1535 A.D., Cairo lost all it gained from the transit trade, when Sultan Selim II agreed to offer France the Decree of Foreign Concessions to protect its merchants and trading houses. Thus French merchants not only sought to protect their own interests, but they also began to impose their will over the Egyptian government and to control its public facilities. Immediately, England – followed by other European states – asked for the same trade agreement that France enjoyed, and these concessions eventually became an obstacle in the development of modern Egypt. This situation prevailed until the foreign concessions were abolished at the Conference of Montreux in the year 1937.

Since the Ottoman rulers made no effort to maintain the city's architectural monuments, the center of Cairo suffered without improvements until the middle of the 19th century. Most of Cairo's districts deteriorated with rare exceptions such as Bab el-Luk, which was isolated by beautiful parks and gardens on one side and a cemetery on the other.

During the 17th and 18th centuries the area of Kanater al-Sebaa (The Lions' Barrages) became overpopulated. It was bordered by the Khalig (the canal) on the west and Berket el-Feil (the elephant's pond) on the east. Between Berket el-Feil and the Citadel, the quarter of Ibn Tulun evolved, with the great mosque in its center. Wealthy residents left the areas close to the Citadel and Sultan Hassan's mosque as a result of repeated rebellions and civil wars. Many houses were destroyed, and others were taken over by vagabonds, while Berket el-Feil and al-Azbakiyah became Cairo's aristocratic sections.

During the 17th and 18th centuries wealthy people built many houses, elegant palaces and gardens on the Nile bank. Many of these palaces still exist, such as the house of el-Sehemi in el-Gamalia that dates from 1648 A.D., the palace of el-Messafer Khana (1789 A.D.), the house of Gamal el-Din el-Dahabi (1637 A.D.), the house of Zainab Khatun, the house of Ibrahim Katkhuda in al-Saiyda Zainab (in Haret Monge) and Bait al-Kredliyah near the mosque of Ibn Tulun.

Below and right: The mosque of Mohammad Ali, known as the Alabaster Mosque for the extensive use of this delicate stone on its interior walls. The mosque was built in 1845 A.D. in proximity to Salah el-Din's Citadel.

The Cairo of *MOHAMMAD ALI* Dr. Morsi Saad El-Din

The opening years of the 19th century found Egypt in a state of chaos and intrigue. A game of politics was in progress between England and France. The Supreme Porte, the name given to the Ottoman caliph, was the cat's paw.

On the other hand, the Mamelukes were working furiously for the possession of power; the Turkish Wali was trying his best to cling to his tottering seat, while Mohammad Ali affected the role of public servant and promoter of public interests. He championed the cause of the *felaheen* (farmers), and mobilized the backing of the *ulamas* of Al-Azhar, because his insight had enabled him to see a source of power – the people – previously untapped and moreover despised by both the Turks and the Mamelukes.

Because the people were convinced that the Mamelukes were the root of all their ills and under the stress of despair, both the people and the *ulamas* took up arms and a revolution ensued. The battles that were supposed to be fought by the French and English were instead fought by the Egyptians themselves.

Sheikhs, *felaheens* and soldiers believed that their salvation from the privation of the rule of the Turkish Wali and the Mamelukes could only be accomplished at the hands of Mohammad Ali. He was their choice, because he was their friend.

When finally in 1805, Mohammad Ali was confirmed by the Porte, the sheikhs retired to their ecclesiastical castle and resumed their teaching duties. The will of the people was asserted, a ruler of their choice was installed, and the foundation stone of Egypt's political structure had been laid. The story of his rise to the throne of Egypt is well known, but the principal feature of the adventure was his insight into the decisive factors of state-building. That insight made him temporarily align himself with the representatives of the Egyptian people to secure their support in his fight for the throne of Egypt; it also enabled him to see that the essence of modern government as represented by Napoleon's Expedition consists of good administration and of the supremacy of the scientific outlook in dealing with problems of policy. Mohammad Ali was a discoverer in a world blind to Western civilization. In putting into effect what he discovered, he achieved real greatness in the history of government.

The deplorable state of the Ottoman Empire made it clear to him that it needed a man of his caliber at its head, and if not at the head of all, at least the head of the Arabic-speaking lands of which Egypt was center. And Napoleon's Expedition to Egypt made it clear that the arts of peace must go side by side with the arts of war. His plan for the monopoly and development of Egypt's agriculture, manufacture and commerce was closely interwoven with his ambitions for expansion.

Having come in on the heels of the French Expedition, he was quick to grasp the attitude of the French, and to pick up the threads of their stifled reforms. Whatever is said about Napoleon's invasion of Egypt and whatever political consequences that invasion had, there is no doubt that in the social and cultural spheres, Egypt benefited greatly.

Napoleon landed at Alexandria on July 1, 1798, and took Cairo within three weeks. The French occupation of Egypt lasted to September 1801, and can be regarded as a turning point in the history of Egypt, launching the country into the modern world.

Although Napoleon was a military man, and although the reasons behind his invasion were purely military and political, he was instrumental in the process of modernization that was later advanced by Mohammad Ali. For Napoleon arrived in Egypt not only at the head of an invading army, but also accompanied by a number of scholars with a view to making scientific research necessary for maintaining rule. It was through those French savants that Egypt for the first time came in touch with modern European thought.

Napoleon showed a real sense of history when he decided to fathom the depth of Egyptian history and civilization. He created a 165-member commission and set them the task of investigating all aspects of Egypt. He also founded "L'Institute de l'Egypte" in August 1798, and its job was twofold. First to discover Egypt, and second to introduce European science into Egypt. The commission produced the famous *La Description de l'Egypte*, which was published in 1822. In the same year, Jean-Francois Champollion published his discoveries about hieroglyphics by scrutinizing the Rosetta Stone, discovered in 1799.

When Mohammad Ali came on the heels of the French in 1801, he continued the process of modernization initiated by the French. This process changed the whole structure of Cairo from a typical Islamic capital to a modern city. In 1801, when the scientists and men of letters evacuated Egypt along with the French troops, they took with them all the documents and the research work they had brought with them. But before they left they were able to create in Egypt, indeed in all the Arab countries, an interest in Western civilization: Mohammad Ali, shrewd as he was, could not fail to realize the importance of diffusing such civilization into his.

His aim was to create from shattered medieval Egypt a

powerful and healthy country, a great, united and independent nation. And he lived to see his aim fulfilled. His first step was to plan a policy of vocational education based on the principle that the country's first need was for qualified candidates to fill up the posts of vital importance. The first two schools established were the Darskhanah to produce Government officials, and the military school at Aswan. These two were followed by a third to train clerks and translators.

القَاهِرَة

Prince Muskau, who found much to admire in Cairo, including the number of fortified castles of the old Mameluke chieftains, which gave the city a feudal appearance, and the "handsome, artificial fountains," said: "The most striking feature of all, however, is the numerous splendid mosques . . . with their high turrets, painted and round windows, their huge masses and the wonderful richness of their innumerable decorations . . . (they) brought to my mind stirring scenes and images of chivalrous valor." During the Prince's visit to Cairo in 1837, Mohammad Ali was building a new mosque, to which he gave his name, to the extreme south of the Citadel opposite the old mosque of Salah el-Din which had fallen into ruins. It was to be "one of the most costly edifices in the world" as its pillars were constructed of polished alabaster and the exterior and interior walls covered with the same material. From the unfinished walls of the mosque the whole of Cairo and beyond – to the distant pyramids of Giza, Dahshur and Saqqara – could be clearly seen. Almost directly below was the beautiful mosque of Sultan Hassan forming a splendid foreground.

One of the most surprising things to those travelers who had made journeys to other eastern cities like Constantinople, Damascus and Teheran was the lack of gardens in Cairo. Carne remarked, "this city is almost without gardens" – different, indeed from the Cairo of today – and Muskau complained that he had to go out to the Pasha's favorite palace at Shubra before he saw a garden worthy of the name. The long road from Cairo to Shubra, built by Mohammad Ali, was a fine avenue. It had been planted with sycamores, forming an arch impenetrable to the sun, and through which the Nile could continually be seen to the left and the desert with its undulating sand-hills to the right. The gardens of Shubra were laid out in the European and Oriental styles. The former consisted of long, graveled walks with little

formal borders and no welcoming shade, but as one writer said, so symmetrical "that George IV would have been delighted to have it at Virginia Water and his English gardens could not have been kept with more neatness and elegance." The Oriental gardens were thickly planted with "myrtles, jessamines, roses, and young orange trees cut to form graceful arcades and festoons." The walks were mosaics of small colored stones, and there was a lake "with splendid marble baths, which are filled by water issuing from crocodiles' mouths." Inside the palace – and most travelers were received by Mohammad Ali who was insatiably curious about all that was going on in the outside world – it was pleasant to sit in the divaned and gilded apartments on rich sofas placed around the windows that looked on to the garden. "The cool rooms offered an agreeable relief from the sultry heat and stifling lanes of Cairo. Here it was easy to fancy that you were entirely in the country."

The reign of Mohammad Ali must have been a wonderful time to visit Cairo. So much was changing, so much was new and the atmosphere was charged with vitality. Trade was flourishing. Cairo was the metropolis of Eastern and African trade. The wares one could buy were innumerable: rare fruit, miniature works of art, turquoises and emeralds, spices, and hippopotamus-hide whips. The caravans from Abyssinia and the Sudan brought gold dust, ivory, rhinoceros' horns, ostrich feathers, gums, and various drugs and medicines. The population, consisting of Arabs, Copts, Turks, Albanians, Greeks, Syrians, Armenians, Jews and "Barbarians from the country beyond the cataracts, in great estimation for their honest industry," numbered in all at the end of Mohammad Ali's reign over a quarter of a million. Never had they enjoyed such tranquility and order.

Most of the travelers were alive to the fact that Egypt was at a turning point in her history. They remarked on the introduction of the cotton plant, the building of a formidable navy, the training of an army of over 100,000 men, the work on the great dam near Cairo, at the beginning of the Delta, of which it was said, "this structure if it succeeds, as it is hoped it will, is likely to surpass almost any undertaking of the kind either ancient or modern." They saw the model school at Kasr el-Aini, a miniature city with modern educational facilities worthy of Cairo, once the seat of Eastern learning.

It is not to be wondered that even the most critical were forced to admit that "changes of unprecedented significance" were taking place before their eyes.

*Below: The ceiling of a Nilometer on the Island of Roda
built to measure the height of the Nile during flood time.
Right: A dam — one of many — built by Mohammad Ali.*

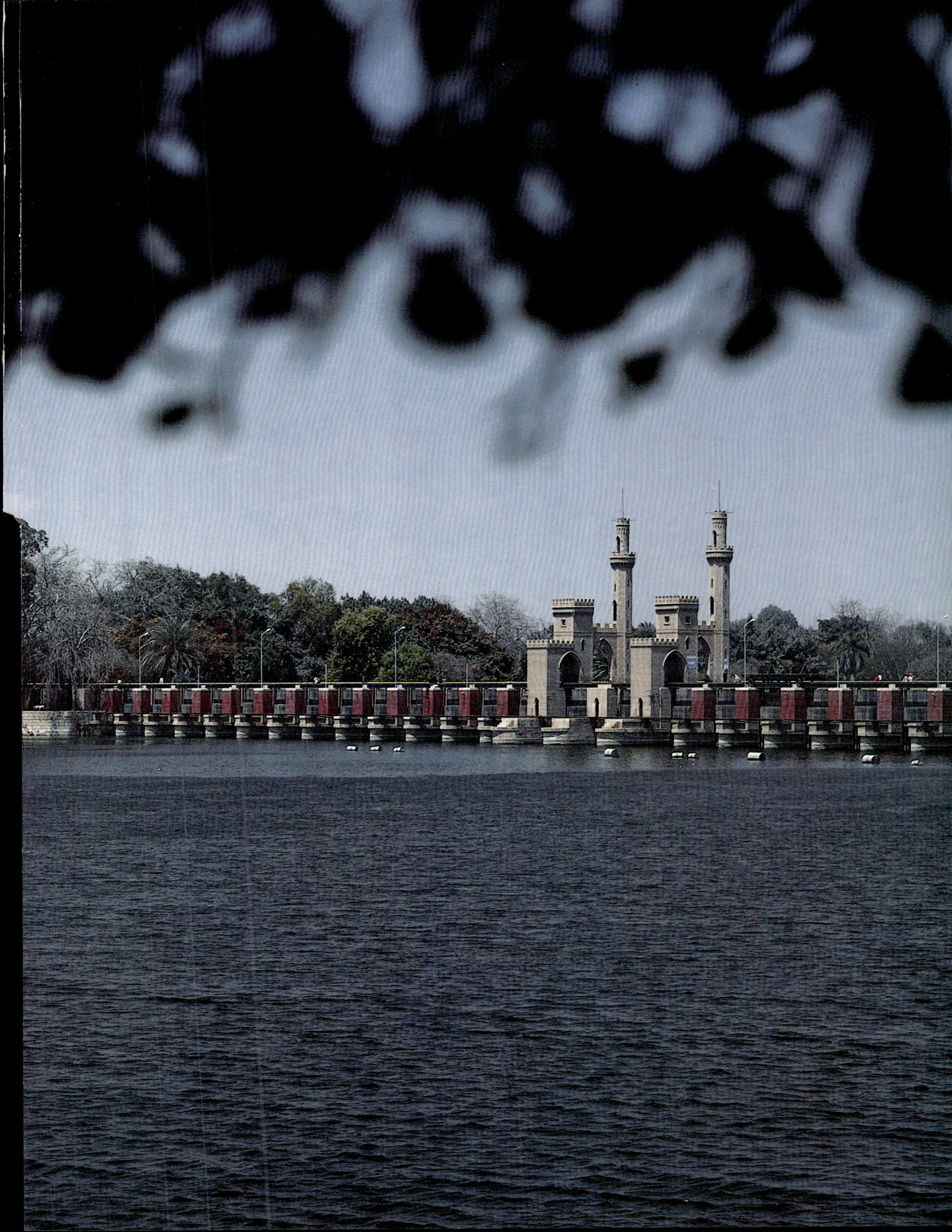

One of the main landmarks of Cairo is the lofty mosque of Mohammad Ali, which is erected high at the southern side of the Citadel, commanding a bird's-eye view of the city equal only to that attained from the top of the Great Pyramid of Giza.

The mosque – known as the Alabaster Mosque for the extensive use of this delicate stone in covering its interior walls – has been described in detail by several architects and many travelers. Needless to say, none of these accounts is by itself complete. Yet gathered together, they all provide excellent material for the study of the elements that cause taste to change in time and space. In addition to this already extensive material is the following translation of an account of this mosque given by the Egyptian architect Ali Mubarak Pasha (1824–1893), who was one of the most brilliant of all Mohammad Ali's mission students. After graduating from the Faculty of Engineering (then called *al-Muhandiskhanah*) he was selected, among others, to complete his military studies in France at the Ecole de Metz. On his return to Egypt in 1849 he was appointed teacher at the Artillery School. In 1871 he became the Minister of Education. His contribution to the Egyptian renaissance is not confined to his great engineering, financial and administrative achievements only, but also to his many literary works for which the most interesting is his history of the Cairo of his time. This work – *al-Khutat al-Tawfikiyya* – written in 20 parts, is still considered one of the sources of Egypt's modern history for the second half of the 19th century. Its first edition, printed at Bulaq, is dated 1305 A.H. (1889–90 A.D.).

In his fifth volume, Ali Mubarak says:

"The mosque was built by the late Hajj (i.e. Pilgrim), Mohammad Ali Pasha, native of Kavala, founder of the Khedivial family in Egypt. He began its erection in the year of the Hejira, 1246 [1830–1831 A.D.], after he had set the affairs of Egypt in order, and completed those operations of vast utility to which we have referred in the introduction of this book. He selected for this mosque a site at the Citadel of Cairo, so that public worship might be enjoyed by the employees in the palace and public offices, since during his time all the ministries and most of the offices were at the Citadel. He prepared for its erection a wide area, around the remains of ruins that had been erected by former kings; he ordered the debris to be cleared away from the site till the solid rock was reached. There, he ordered the foundations of his mosque to be laid. He built a foundation of enormous stones, some three and a half meters in length; iron rods, welded with molten lead, connected each pair of stones. In this way, the foundations were laid till the surface of the ground was reached. The mosque was modeled on a mosque in Constantinople, called Lur

Osman, and on that of Sidi Sariyah in the Citadel. The building was continued in the style described. Four doors were made, two to the north, one admitting to the court, the other to the dome; two also were placed on the south side. The stone walls were completely faced with alabaster both on the inside and the outside. He who enters from the gate of the Citadel called Bab al-Daris finds a large court and the dome. The door leading into the court has an inscription in gilt on marble, a text from the Quran commending prayer. The threshold is of marble, the door of antique wood; the tympanum is of wood also. The height of the door is four meters, the wooden tympanum is one meter high. The wall is two meters thick. The court is 57 meters long by 55 wide, its surface being 3.135 square meters. It embraces five iwans, surmounted by 47 domes, mounted on marble pillars, eight meters high, exclusive of the base. The number of these pillars which surround the court and support the domes is 45. Each has a necking and torus of brass, and each column is connected with another by an iron bar making 94 bars in all. From each dome a brass chain is appended to which a lamp is attached. As one enters this door, one finds on the left the door of the minaret made of ordinary wood; 265 steps lead to the summit, exclusive of those which lead up to the iron obelisk which crowns it. On the left side in the middle, between the two iwans, is the door which leads from the court into the dome; it consists of folding doors of antique wood with a semi-circular tympanum; over it the date is written in Turkish. Some seven yards in front of the iwan next to the door of the dome is the door which leads to the second minaret, ascended by the same number of steps as the first; they both form winding staircases with bronze balustrades. On every door a text from Surat al-Fath is engraved. The height of each of these minarets is 84 meters from the ground to the iron summit, of which 25 and $^2/_3$ of which are from the floor to the roof of the mosque. On the left-hand side are the nine windows of the dome, heading each of which a text from the Surat al-Fath is engraved in marble and gilded. The door of the dome is decorated with a text promising Paradise to believers. In the middle of the court you find a wooden dome mounted on eight marble columns, seven meters high, and underneath there is a fountain with an alabaster cupola and 16 spouts, with a marble spout over each, decorated with texts from the Quran. In front of each spout there is a marble base. Between each pair of pillars there is an iron rod, holding a brass chain for a lamp, and over each is a crescent of bronze. Close by is the entrance to the cistern which is underneath the court; the coping is of alabaster and the lid of brass, and there is a pump for raising water.

"The gate of the southern court faces that of the northern, and both are alike. . . . In the iwans which surround the court there are 38 windows, two and a half meters in length and one and a half in breadth; the thickness of the wall is two meters. It also has one window in bronze. In front of the north door which gives on to the dome you find a gallery on 24 alabaster columns,

with bronze neckings and tori, each eight meters high, not including the base. The pillars are connected by 22 iron bars, and surmounted by 11 domes with bronze crescents. . . . Hence you proceed into the sanctuary, which is almost square, 46 meters by 45, exclusive of the iwan of the qibla, which is 17 meters by nine, covering an area of 135 meters. There you find a very lofty dome, some 61 meters above the floor of the mosque, mounted on four piers of hewn stone, faced with marble to a height of two meters. The dome has four semi-circles, one on each side, and four small domes. The whole of the great dome is elaborately painted and decorated with gold leaf. . . . There are circles painted round it, with some texts from the Quran inscribed in gold leaf. To the left of the sanctuary you find the mihrab, with a semi-circular roofing, while the niche itself is in marble with an inscription in colored glass. The niche is enclosed between two small marble columns with brass necking and torus. To the left, close to one of the piers that have been mentioned, is the reader's chair made of wood, with a carved balustrade. Five steps lead up to it and it is carpeted in red. To the right is the pulpit made of wood and decorated with gold leaf, reached by 25 steps, also carpeted in red and with folding doors. Above in a circle texts are also inscribed. Above the preacher's seat is an oblong dome on four wooden columns with a Quranic text written round it. At the bottom of the pulpit there is a wicket on each side, inscribed with texts; between them there is a sort of cupboard to which access is given by a door under the pulpit. Facing the mihrab is the door of the dome leading out of the court, surmounted by a dikka for the mu'azen, extending the whole breadth of the sanctuary, and mounted on eight marble pillars, eight meters high, surrounded by a bronze balustrade, which also surrounds the upper part of the sanctuary; this upper part has 31 windows with brass frames and white glass. At a distance of about 12 meters there is another balustrade, with 31 more windows, of stained glass. Between the two there are the 24 windows of the great dome, with brass balustrade, and bronze work with stained glass lights, and the balustrade at the top of the dome has in front of it 40 stained glass windows. Round each of the four domes mentioned above there are 10 windows with balustrades. The purpose of these balustrades is to support lamps. In the semi-circle of the mihrab there are windows, with a balustrade gallery, and round the wall low down there are 36 windows, two and a half meters long, with white glass lights, a portion of the poem 'Burdah' being written on each one. Access is given to the galleries from the two minarets and the roof of the mosque. The southern door of the dome, which faces the northern, has written on the outside: 'To God belong the places of worship.' In front is a spacious gallery, on 11 columns of alabaster, some eight meters high, with 22 iron bars connecting them; these are surmounted by 11 domes, similar to those in the gallery facing the first door.

"*The mosque was thus completed in the year 1261 A.H. [1845 A.D.].*"

Like all historical figures, Mohammad Ali has his antagonists and proponents. He is accused by the former of being a military dictator, which, for all intents and purposes, he was. The latter accede that he was a dictator, but a benevolent one who suddenly transformed Egypt from the Middle Ages to the modern world.

If we justly weigh the gains and losses during his reign, Mohammad Ali will be remembered as the initiator of the process that made Cairo what it is now, the mother of the world.

Dr. Morsi Saad El-Din

الهويّة